World in Crisis

WORLD IN CRISIS

THE END OF THE AMERICAN CENTURY

GABRIEL KOLKO

ARBEITER RING PUBLISHING · WINNIPEG

Copyright © 2009 Gabriel Kolko

Arbeiter Ring Publishing
201E-121 Osborne Street
Winnipeg, Manitoba
Canada R3L 1Y4
www.arbeiterring.com

Printed in Canada by Transcontinental Printing

Cover by Terry Corrigan
This book is a co-edition with Pluto Press, UK.

With assistance of the Manitoba Arts Council/Conseil des Arts du Manitoba.

We acknowledge the support of the Canada Council for our publishing program.

ARP acknowledges the financial support to our publishing activities of the Manitoba Arts Council/Conseil des Arts du Manitoba, Manitoba Culture, Heritage and Tourism, and the Government of Canada through the Book Publishing Industry Development Program (BPIDP).

Printed on 100% recycled paper.

Library and Archives Canada Cataloguing in Publication

Kolko, Gabriel
    World in crisis: end of the American century / Gabriel Kolko.

Includes index.
ISBN 978-1-894037-39-6

    1. United States—Foreign relations—2001-. 2. United States—Military policy. 3. United States—Politics and government—2001-. 4. World politics—1995-2005. 5. World politics—2005-2015. 6. Balance of power. I. Title.

E895.K66 2009   327.73009'051   C2008-906923-4

To integrity and reason

And to Joyce

Contents

Introduction

This is about the world as it is, not how it should be. How the world should be is simple enough to articulate but at this stage virtually impossible to realize.

The international order is again breaking down at astonishing speed, accelerated by the collapse of "communism" and the Soviet bloc. Back then, the enemy was clear: there was a Cold War against the USSR's "evil empire." Now it is the indefinable "terrorist," who exists in the Middle East, in Africa – everywhere. There is today far more instability than there was in 1991, and nuclear proliferation has made the world far more dangerous. The conventional wisdom inherited from the Cold War era is now irrelevant. Dangers have not only increased but lines have been blurred. Understanding reality is today far more difficult. In that process, American power – and the century it dominated – is declining irretrievably. What follows is an attempt to explain this process.

There is no longer any opposition, and no illusions – not only on the Left but also among those who favor the existing "capitalist" system, which label describes countless variations of the exploitation of humans by other humans. The world ceased being ideological in the 1980s, at the latest, and the practices – economic above all – of all nations now fall within quite similar, predictable parameters. However they describe themselves, economic inequality exists in all nations.

At the very moment at which there was need for an opposition, the socialist movement disappeared, de facto or

1

formally. Religion and endless forms of obscurity are now more than likely to fill the immense vacuum created by the death of naive socialist ideologies promising the salvation of mankind's economic fate and by the abysmal failure of capitalist theory. Instead, the option is far more likely to be irrationality and atavism.

But capitalism is destroying itself. There is simply no longer a force ready to replace it, and yet it is losing immense sums of money. Its malaises and crises will be with us for many years, to be endured for as long as the people of the world accept its consequences. Perhaps a new opposition will emerge. One may hope there is time for it to do so, even though that appears less and less likely.

For while anti-capitalists – Leftists if you will – cannot make any predictions on the future of history, neither can those who favor or defend the status quo of capitalism tell us what will occur tomorrow or next year. The future is open, and this intriguing dynamism ensures that history remains open too. The Right suffers from the same blindness and myopia as the Left; and while this was also true of the experiences of past centuries, in relation to the limits of contemporary American power it is especially crucial. All predictions have failed, and empires have fallen along with dreams of a utopian, ideal future. In this regard the United States is not exempt from the vagaries of time. Its turn has come.

Ours is an age of growing chaos, of cynicism and disillusion. As Zbigniew Brzezinski, President Jimmy Carter's National Security Adviser, put it at the beginning of 2008: "we are now in a phase in which all of mankind is politically activated and restless."[1] Most of the turmoil has existed from the Sinai Peninsula to the Indian Ocean, from western China to South Russia – a vast area. Upheavals and instability have been greatest in this immense region but scarcely restricted to it. This increasingly turbulent world has also increasingly unified around one issue: fear or hatred – or both – of the United States.

Capitalism is in a growing crisis and the century of American domination is ending – perhaps it has ended already. Even in the absence of any viable opposition, American capitalism is tending towards committing suicide – and is taking other nations with it.

The following chapters offer my recent thoughts on the decline of American power and the destruction of the institutions that are crucial to it, on NATO and the US-led alliance, on Iran and Iraq, Israel, and the global financial structure. Originally intended to be a collection of recent articles, in many instances new developments have compelled me to add to and revise the texts, often very substantially, since the world is today changing at a breathtaking pace and telescoping events are transforming the conditions that existed when my original essays were written. The outcome is a series of chapters with often scant resemblance to the original articles but united by a common theme: the decline of American power, the limits of its military technology, and the end of a century in which the United States had the pretension to lead the world.

Though my focus is on recent history, there is a continuum of which the present crises are but a part. It is true that today's changes and policies appear to be qualitatively different to those of earlier episodes. But the changes are those of degree, not kind, even if what occurs now is irrational or leads to unexpected results. In crucial respects, it is the continuum that deserves much greater emphasis, but the artificial exercise of dealing with the present can never obscure the ways in which there are key precedents for virtually everything that has occurred since 2004. This continuity is intellectual, organizational, political, and implemented by very ambitious people who often do not believe in anything but success. Opportunism – everywhere – is far more crucial than ideology in determining what people say and do. A nation, and above all its military, cannot make rational decisions when their policies are determined by elites composed of ambitious men and women – as they are in most cases – rather than motivated by a disinterested intelligence or an impersonal sense of "honor."

I often refer to these past events because there is continuity in all modern history. The origins of most of the world's problems go back many centuries and involve religion, boundaries, demography, economic expansion, nationalism – the list of causes of war and human misery is very long. The US has hardly been the only cause of most of them, and America scarcely has a monopoly on stupidity or venality. But even granted that international politics had been messed up for a very long time, after World War II the role of the US became decisive most places on the globe. Had Washington behaved differently after 1945 the world would be very different than it is today. In short, the "American problem" became synonymous with the international political problem, such that virtually everything important involving international change is now contingent on solving it.

Since 1945 the US has poured fuel on the fire of atavism and irrationality, and has blocked efforts to solve the domestic problems of countless nations. It is worth contemplating what might have happened had it minded its own affairs and avoided making complex situations far worse – much less undoing efforts to reform them. I have devoted one book to America's interventions in the Third World alone, another to the Vietnam War, and dealt with many other cases elsewhere. While I have been comprehensive in the continents I cover, I have here left out many examples of US interference with the processes and dynamics of political and economic change in many nations and its attempts everywhere – from Latin America to Africa, Asia, and the Middle East – to alter the direction of events in ways both congenial to American ambitions and vital for its economic and geopolitical interests. There are innumerable excellent and detailed works that go much further. Still, while I am engaging here only in description and analysis, there is nonetheless great value in also considering alternatives to those we are now saddled with.

While we could begin our speculation anywhere, the situation in the Muslim world – predominantly the Middle East but also Pakistan – is for the time being the preeminent crisis facing the US and the world as a whole. The territorial settlements imposed on the Middle East after 1918 were arbitrary, unjust, and regulated entirely by the great powers with scant regard for local conditions, religious tendencies or desires. An astonishing ignorance prevailed among most of the crucial decision-makers, and not just the Americans. While Islamic influences and secular nationalism existed in tandem, as did the persistence of tribalism, foreign intervention was decisive in shaping the political and economic nature of the entire region. It still is. At the inception – World War I and the peace settlement that followed – the United States was important, but Great Britain and France were decisive.

We might begin anywhere in the region but since I have written about it before Iran offers the most convenient starting point. Nonetheless, to have begun with Iraq or Palestine and Israel – and I am personally quite familiar with the latter

– would have been just as pertinent. I should make it clear that I regard the Afghan and Iraq wars as great disasters in American history, wars that will persist and color its politics for years to come – unless (as I believe they are likely to) they become too expensive and protracted in time to endure. But there are multiple causes of America's decline and while I assess here what I believe to be the crucial elements of that demise, I can scarcely claim to have covered them all.

World War II also vindicated the fears of those who argued that the peace settlements reached after the first war would only lead to a new crisis, and today most of the Islamic world is in flames or perilously unstable as a consequence of those settlements. The roots of the problem there can be traced in large part to the way the vast region's nations and borders were created capriciously after World War I; in no area was the potential for chaos – the unresolved boundaries, and the creation of a Jewish homeland – greater than in the inherently volatile area stretching from the Mediterranean to South Asia, in which there are no "natural" nations and boundaries, cultural or physical. By attacking Iraq the US has reopened a potential for chaos and disorder in the entire region which exceeds, by far, the stakes which existed in Indochina, Brazil, or any place else where the US has mucked around. For while there were plenty of illusions surrounding American intervention in such places, the disorder the US is now creating in the Muslim world is in fact unprecedented. It could have been far different had the America not tried to control the fate of this immense region at all.

Iran presented the first major crisis for the US in the Middle East. Crises concerning "communism" in Europe and China may have preceded it, but the Soviet Union's demise after 1991 removed the illusion that the issue was one of ideology rather than simply power. Emphasizing the US commitment to aggrandizing its power rather than to anti-communism is a crucial point because, while the US was certainly anti-communist, at least the Soviet Union offered a major element of stability and predictability which was to disappear in 1991. Russia today – still possessing a vast quantity of nuclear bombs and exporting the most modern weapons – is virtually America's enemy. Focusing on power, rather than anti-communism, is a far better way to understand the goals of US foreign policy. The US demonization of communism was ultimately a convenient facade.

In Iran the US was utterly opportunist. It brought the Shah to power essentially as an absolute ruler, but was eager to work with Islamic fundamentalists to throw out Mossadegh, a democratically elected middle-class secular nationalist – a bourgeois if you will – who was intending to modify existing oil contracts and thereby damage British interests. The CIA and British plan for overthrowing Mossadegh provided for using a "religious cover" for political demonstrations designed to "reinforce the backbone of the Shah." The mullahs and clerics were to play a vital role in the coup, and pass judgment on the "orthodoxy" of all legislation.[2] Washington encouraged Muslim fundamentalists as a presumed antidote to communism for the next four decades. It also encouraged the weakening of British power in the region and the rise of American influence – and oil interests – in the Middle East.

In late September 2003 President George Bush declared to the world that "our responsibility to history is already clear: to answer these attacks and the world of evil." Terrorism, coming mainly from radicalized Muslims, was trying to destroy our "way of life." Since then the United States has become the world's most feared and hated nation; it is in the process of losing two protracted, vastly expensive wars, and jihadists throughout the Islamic world have become far stronger. These wars are also helping to bankrupt the American economy – aided, of course, by the epidemic of greed and innovation among American and world finance and banking institutions.

It has also produced an alienation – almost a form of radicalization – among diverse constituencies, ranging from hitherto loyal bureaucrats in the International Monetary Fund and World Bank to American military officers. Those who upheld the virtues of the old order now realize how dangerous it has become and how empty their principles now are. These people have not turned to the traditional Left, social democracy or communism, but they have ceased to believe in the system and have become profoundly unhappy. Suicide rates among American military personnel since the Iraq War began have moved into the stratosphere. By 2005 they accounted for fully a fifth of all US suicides. And that is only the tip of the iceberg. Americans are increasingly beginning to resent their government's foreign policies.

But what the United States does in foreign affairs has always been intimately linked to financial and economic issues and to the health of capitalism. The ultimate constraint on it is the limit of its resources, which, while very great, are finite. Its resources are economic but also restricted in terms of manpower and the confusion of its priorities. If what is projected to be a small affair, as in Vietnam, becomes much larger, its ability to confront problems where the stakes are far more important – as in Latin America today – are constrained, and priorities start to become determined in response to where the most shooting is occurring. The "credibility" of US armed power then becomes a fixation, one that ensures the persistence or escalation of a conflict long after what was intended to be a small affair in a region of no special importance to US interests should have been abandoned.

This means that virtually everything the US does internationally is potentially important because it inevitably confronts unexpected surprises. This in turn imposes a potentially vast analytic task on us – we must understand a great deal, virtually everything, because what seems like a small escapade for the US tends to move center stage. The decision-makers in Washington are quite blind to the potential consequences of their smallest actions. Again, while Vietnam proved this, it is happening again today in Iraq and other regions. And overriding all that the US does is the health of its economy, which imposes constraints that can be decisive. This has occurred in the cases of both the Vietnam and Iraq wars, both of which were seen as "limited" affairs that would be over quite quickly.

America's behavior – like that of many other nations – also reflects the career aspirations of top bureaucrats, civilian and military, who wish to "get ahead" and rise within the system – a mentality that prevents policies based on rational reflection and makes careerism the dominant impulse. At the present time, it could not be worse for America because the financial structure is teetering in ways that are awesome – and changing for the worse every day.

The world economic context for American foreign-policy adventurism has rarely, perhaps never, been so dismal. There is global gloom, the central banks are confused and increasingly impotent, hedge funds and investments houses are closing shop after making huge losses in the billions, and far worse is likely to come. "New kids on the block," the sovereign wealth funds of the oil-rich states, from the Persian

Gulf to Russia, as well as China, are awash with money and threaten to use it as a political and policy instrument. There are surprises every day and it is becoming an adventure in itself to read the financial news. Growing pessimism reigns among supporters of the system: official monetary agencies as well as journalists and private investors are reaching a dour consensus.

In the end, states are going to pay out hundreds of billions – perhaps trillions – of dollars for these losses, as they once again come to the rescue of the businessmen who have played and lost. And these sums will be added to the costs of a foreign policy already far too expensive. The contradictions of the economy will meet the immense costs of adventures abroad, and American power will inevitably decline; its century of hubris will come to an end.

Capitalism in the United States has invented huge losses, thereby changing the world scene. Nominally, it began with home mortgages, but that only escalated problems already in the system, producing a general unraveling. Greed, an institutional structure, and new ways of making – and losing – money among banks, investment houses, and the like, only built on a base that was fragile already, leaving the US far more vulnerable in coping with the new emergency. Earlier, well before the home-mortgage crisis, it suffered from immense balance-of-payments deficits, excess Treasury borrowings, wars in Afghanistan and Iraq, a dollar that has fallen against the euro almost 60 percent from 2002 to April 2008 and its decline as a reserve currency, and much else besides. Likewise, US dependence on imports for two-thirds of its petroleum needs leaves it exceedingly vulnerable.

Today the US is far weaker in coping with the latest financial emergencies, which nominally began in the summer of 2007 but are the consequences of two decades of laxity euphemistically called deregulation and globalization. Europe too has suffered from the post-2007 crises but was in a far stronger position than America to resist them. The cost of being a part of a trading system, which the United States leads, is now far too high. These economic problems are cascading.

I could go on ad infinitum giving reasons why the American century is ending. But ending it is – and with it the vast informal empire constructed after 1914. American military manpower is utterly inadequate for its global mission. In Iraq alone it needs 300,000 troops to secure Baghdad – virtually twice the number the United States has in the entire country, where it now must confront armed Shiites in the most remote places. The war in Iraq, though, is "a major debacle," to cite the Pentagon's National Defense University in April 2008, and likely to be lost.

Apart from the fact that pursuit of power, not anti-communism, is the motive of US global impulses, there is another reason why American power is no longer viable. While the same can be said for other nations at various points in their history, the existing American system has the fundamental problem that it cannot be run according to rational criteria, and, like Marxism, it has no "laws." Every branch of life – the military, the political structure, culture – is filled with adventurers, opportunists, egomaniacs, psychotics, destructive types and the like, who make or accept disorder. The hypocrisy of politicians, since time immemorial and in all places, makes skepticism towards their pretensions – whether they call themselves aristocrats, capitalists, or socialists – the only safe position.

George W. Bush may possibly be the worst president in American history, but it has always had bad presidents – some worse than others. After all, there were potholes in most American highways long before Bush was elected and the American government instead preferred to ensure its military was the best armed in the world. Bush inherited priorities that made his skewed society possible, but he was scarcely unique or unprecedented.

For these and numerous other reasons, the United States is prone to make basic mistakes that threaten its very stability. Capitalism in every nation self-destructs because of innovations and greed, not "laws." Military leaders and politically ambitious men and women say whatever will advance their careers and not what they really think or believe. People who are socialists in their youth become cynics. Opportunism is the rule. There is no organized class-conscious proletariat in the US or elsewhere, but neither is there a capitalist rationality, an ability to operate or control the system by "objective" standards, because the pervasiveness of greed and ambition makes a higher logic and rationality impossible.

The end result is intense, growing dissatisfaction at home, while the United States has become the world's most hated nation abroad – hated above all by Muslims, who have replaced "communists" as America's enemy of choice. Of 22 national populations at the beginning of 2008, 39 percent favored immediate US withdrawal from Iraq and 28 percent wanted withdrawal within a year. Only 23 percent believed the US should persist until security improves. By August 2007, 24 percent of the American population wanted immediate withdrawal from Iraq and 35 percent supported withdrawal within a year. Since then the percentage has become yet higher. There is now a financial disorder of a type unprecedented since the 1930s, wars the United States cannot win and refuses to acknowledge as lost, and the transformation of interventionism abroad into madness. Hence the end of the American century.

We live, instead, in an increasingly complex, interconnected age, which is almost surrealist – with virtually everything involving the economy within the US or internationally being interrelated and beyond the control of anybody, whether individuals or nations. Nuclear proliferation is occurring and no one knows how many nations have nuclear weapons, but it is fundamental to America's decline. Everything challenges our comprehension. And it is changing at a breathtaking speed that makes all generalizations on war and peace or the American and world economy contingent and liable to change, even tomorrow.

As fascinating as the details may be, the general patterns and interrelationships are my ultimate focus. This short volume consists of some of the many articles I have written since 2004, virtually all of them revised, since keeping pace with reality demanded that one set them in a broader context. They deal with the limits of American power and those of its allies, especially Israel, in a context that is changing constantly, and that will continue to do so.

Our task is to understand reality, and once we do we have a realistic basis for changing it. Hence the essays and comments that follow.

1
The Financial Crisis

The problem with writing about the world economy and finance, and the causes of the present global crisis, is that each day's news makes what preceded it seem almost irrelevant. It is impossible to keep up with the topic ... or the losses. Is it a trillion dollars, as the International Monetary Fund (IMF) predicted it would be in early 2008? Or is it far more, as others have since contended? The world economy and finance presents the most obscure and complex problem for everyone: both the intellectually radical and those who have power and money to gain or to lose. For the rich it is the key question facing them every day. Others, like myself, are just curious – these problems are abstract.

Since at least 1914, American foreign policy has always been related in some crucial manner to the state of the economy. Economics perplexes all men and women of power; it is the ultimate constraint on them whatever their nationality – the arbiter of what they can and cannot do. The US war in Vietnam led to inflation and the bleeding of its gold reserves, and that was one vital reason it lost the conflict there. The international influence of the US, its universal mission since 1947 to organize the world's affairs, has been based in large part on its economic strength. Hence the present discussion precedes everything that follows because a panorama of the state of the economy – American and international – is essential. The wars in the Middle East and Afghanistan, whatever the reasons for them, have helped fuel the vertiginous rise in the price of oil, a situation that now gives the war in Iraq, and the possibility of war between the US and Iran, a special significance. It has also greatly accelerated the loss of American power.

Then there is the decline of the role of the US dollar, and America's critical national debt of almost $10 trillion, most of it owed the Arab states, China, and countries it assumes it can instruct on everything from women's rights to political morality despite the fact its economic growth rate today falls behind – far behind in most cases – the rest of the major industrial nations. China now has the largest foreign currency reserve of any nation in the world – $1.5 trillion as of the end of 2007 – and immense political influence as a result. Since much of this is invested in US Treasury notes, the threat of withdrawal of that investment gives China strong leverage over American actions.

There is also the continuous deficit on the United States' balance of goods and services, due to its petroleum consumption (which is overwhelmingly dependent on imports), and its growing penchant for imported automobiles, toys, and garments made in China, etc. From 1997, when the US was already in deficit, to 2006, the deficit on goods and services increased sevenfold, and by 2006 its balance on goods was a stupendous $838 billion in the red. When George W. Bush arrived in the White House in 2001 there was a surplus in federal receipts, outlays, and debt. It took him one year to create a deficit, which by 2008 – following the wars in Afghanistan and Iraq – amounted to $400 billion. The Iraq War will cost the US nearly $3 trillion, according to testimony given the US Congress Joint Economic Committee in June 2008.

As a consequence, the euro is replacing the US dollar as the basic global reserve currency. The trade-weighted dollar depreciated at an annualized rate of ten percent between 2002 and mid 2007. With it came the decline of American power.

While the nature of the world financial structure is significant in itself, it is also highly relevant to contemporary American foreign policy. But we must first consider some of the key reasons for the present financial crisis. Globalization and the "Washington consensus," with its emphasis on free trade and minimal state intervention in the "market," initially meant that massive corporations and banks in the US and other leading economies were able to extend their power and increase profits by expanding their interests in poorer nations. But globalization and world economic interdependence has to a certain degree become self-defeating, with the spread of ways to lose money on a grand scale, as well as make it. In addition to sending troops overseas, American money was the principal cause of the globalization process, but it remains to be seen whether the losses outweigh the gains from the massive US export of capital and investment in the post-1945 period.

Between 2001 and 2006, interest rates in the US were so low that American banks loaned money to financial adventurers, with the consequence that these banks and investment funds are now losing immense sums of money. This new breed of adventurer may or may not have been independent of the traditional financial elite, which had shown no reluctance to provide them with the funds they required, but they created a new kind of international finance quite unlike that which had hitherto existed, making and losing enormous sums of money in ways which bore little relation to the traditional operations of the real economy. From the inception of modern capitalism, ground-breaking individuals – from Andrew Carnegie, John D. Rockefeller, and Henry Ford up to Bill Gates – were considered "outsiders." Their success was due to technological innovation, the invention of new products and processes, new forms of organization, and the like. But throughout these innovations, the modern capitalist economy always endured.

The buccaneers of the past 20 years operated in new ways that brought them huge rewards – such that the number of billionaires in the world has increased more than fivefold since 1998 – but that were also far more dangerous. As a consequence, capitalism has become unstable – how unstable remains to be seen. But capitalism will persist if only because there is no real alternative, socialist or otherwise, to replace it. Instead, chaos and huge losses will most likely endure.

In several countries capitalism is today vulnerable, perhaps fatally, to an economic crisis that is an international phenomenon, profoundly affecting many nations simultaneously. Capitalism has of course undergone crises since the seventeenth century, but there is a fundamental difference today. Economies are now interdependent to a degree that is unique – exposed to each others' foibles, weakened by virtue of being reliant on each other in ways that have never before been the case. Both investment patterns and the impact of information and communication technologies have created crises endemic in the system. Esteemed credit rating services have ranked highly precarious financial devices as being safe, while naive investors of every sort, including investment funds, have lost billions of dollars.

There are explanations – however dated – and the origin of the present crisis is not a mystery. The rest of the subjects covered in this book move quickly too, but nothing is as surprising and unpredictable as the world economic structure, and it may be decisive in determining what happens in Iraq, the Middle East, indeed everywhere.

The problems began with the assumption, inherited from nineteenth-century ideologies, that the economy was self-correcting, the product of impersonal forces and instincts. The result over the past 50 years has been that deregulation and privatization have gradually become comprehensive, although regulation has been retained or modified whenever it has suited the interests of powerful businesses.

From its inception – roughly 1887 – regulation in the US has entailed providing some faction of business with what it needs or demands. Politically based regulation was resorted to when companies failed in stabilizing their branch of economic activity through merger movements, and when there was too much competition. The notion of there being some abstract "public interest" at stake was a myth concealing a regulatory process designed to save those nominally regulated with measures intended to save railroads, bankers, and industrialists from losses. If losses continued to occur – as they often did – it was because regulators frequently lacked the understanding of what concrete measures were required, such that American railroads and banks have repeatedly required further new legislation. What exact steps will suffice often defy those who have the best intentions but do not know how to proceed.

The reality over the past decades is that bankers and investors were increasingly free to do as they liked – including inventing endless ways to lose money. Credit default swaps scarcely existed in 2000; in 2007 they were in excess of $60 trillion. Some creations, like CDS insurance on bond defaults, were sheer bets – gambling involving trillions of dollars. And they are but one of many such creations. That, in brief, is how we got to where we are today.

The problem arose in large part because bankers and investment houses created much of the financial chaos, and the International Monetary Fund was established in mid 1944 to regulate only national economies, not the operations of private financial institutions. But today all of the international institutions created after World War II have become increasingly passé, if not obsolete. The new global economic reality is very different to the one assumed when the Bretton Woods system was created. Risk, called "innovation," has been a part of capitalism since it began, but it has been growing since 1970 and increasing in complexity every decade. Today it is more convoluted than it has ever been, both in the United States and the rest of the world, and far beyond what was once considered conventional economic activity.

Central banks, and the governments that ultimately control them, must find solutions, and they cannot because they have rarely, if ever, agreed on anything consequential. They disagree on virtually everything important – as they did in the 1920s. Central banks have increasing problems and the solutions they propose, as in the past, will be utterly inadequate, not because their intentions are wrong but because it is impossible to regulate such a vast, complex world economy – even less so today than in the past because there is no agreed-upon international mechanism for such regulation in place. The powerful nations all regard regulation jealously, and the US system is totally incompatible with all of them. The financial crisis that began in 2007 was confronted, if it was confronted at all, by national regulatory bodies. In an era of financial globalization, it was merely a matter of time before the recent exotic financial innovations merged into a crisis that transcended borders and inflicted far greater damage to national economies. Internationalization of finance has meant less regulation than ever, and regulation was scarcely very effective even at the national level.

Central banks are now free to give advice, in the very unlikely case they can agree, and the bankers and investment houses are usually equally free to ignore it. But even if the banks agreed, the new finance system is far too complex to be regulated, especially in the US, where states and the federal government have competing regulations. Finance – and its control – has been increasingly privatized and is increasingly unregulated altogether. Banks have invented ways to move trillions in assets off their books – permitting them to make money but also to hide massive losses in the trillions of dollars. Perhaps it will become many trillions. We shall see. The banks admitted this in the spring of 2008, in large part because there was no doubt about their losing vast sums and they were determined to head off onerous regulation.

The entire international mechanism based on nation states is now irrelevant – the IMF included. The massive financial losses have now spread to industrial corporations, affecting their health also, and made the entire world economy much more precarious. Capitalism is now free, including in ways that make it more and more self-destructive – or at least unprofitable.

In this context, the influence of all the 1944 Bretton Woods-created international banks, the IMF in particular, has been greatly reduced, and their core premises are increasingly rejected, both by nations and within their own organizations – above all because of the rising price of commodities and the remarkable economic rise of India and China. But US power was based, to a great extent, on the role these Washington-based institutions played. With their decline, American power is going with them. Nations that prevailed over the US, like Vietnam, subsequently tailored their economic policies to suit IMF and World Bank prescriptions – giving the US, at least symbolically, the ultimate victory in the Vietnam War despite the fact that its weapons proved ineffective. In the case of China, its "communist" period was temporary, and it has since developed into a dynamic economic power, despite its mixture of private capitalism and statism, such that the US now fears it more than ever.

The IMF warned in April 2008 that the US mortgage crisis beginning in the summer of 2007 has become "the largest financial shock since the Great Depression." "The world economy has entered new and precarious territory." Emerging nations such as China and India are now the motors of growth, the price of oil and commodities has increased steeply, and the American current account deficit has grown dramatically, further weakening a dollar already under great strain from the cost of wars in Afghanistan and Iraq. A global recession – perhaps a depression similar to that of the 1930s – is now possible unless policy-makers "continue strong efforts to deal with financial market turmoil to avoid a full-blown crisis of confidence or a credit crunch."[1] The IMF's odds of a one-in-four chance of a major crisis occurring are purely speculative. We shall see.

What began as a sub-prime mortgage market involving a mere $34 billion in troubled loans had by the summer of 2007 imperiled a $57 trillion American financial system and then spread to numerous nations throughout the globe. Wall Street banks and investment houses – not to mention those in Paris,

London, and Zurich – had utilized countless techniques of financial engineering, most of the highest risk and involving leverage, employing all forms of credit, collateralized debts, and the like to partition mortgage debts into risk segments. Investment instruments of every sort, too numerous to mention, are losing money. Some of the biggest banks and investment houses, once deemed prudent institutions, are losing vast sums and may lose far more. The names may change, but they include well-known firms as well as obscure companies. Their identities are less important than the fact that greed was the only motive behind their recourse to exotic financial devices which, while they generated gains for many years, have now created an economic crisis without parallel.

Meanwhile, the IMF wants taxpayers to rescue the banks and investment houses by way of national treasuries taking over mortgage-backed assets to prevent falling housing prices from creating a vicious circle, leading to fresh blows to the world's banks and spiraling into a precarious feedback that will endanger the entire global investment system. This approach would, in effect, socialize the losses. And such a rescue is likely to occur in many sectors of the financial structure on the premise that they are too big, and well-connected, to be allowed to fail. The taxpayers will pick up the bill and greed will not be penalized. Losses, in effect, will be socialized for the sake of those who are against socialism.

WEAPONS OF MASS FINANCIAL DESTRUCTION
(Le Monde Diplomatique, October 2006)

The global financial structure is far less transparent now than it has ever been. A few decades ago daily payments for foreign exchange transactions were roughly equivalent to the capital stock of a major US bank; today they exceed the combined capital of the top 100 US banks. Financial adventurers constantly create new products that defy nation states and international banks. In May 2006 the IMF's managing director, Rodrigo de Rato, deplored these new risks, which the weakness of the US dollar and the US's mounting trade deficits have greatly magnified.

De Rato's fears reflect the fact that the IMF has been in both structural and intellectual crisis. Structurally, its outstanding credit and loans have declined sharply since 2003, from over $70 billion to a little over $20 billion, leaving it with far less leverage over the economic policies of developing nations, and a smaller income than its expensive operations require. The IMF admits it has been "quantitatively marginalized."[2] Many of its problems are due to the doubling since 2003 of world prices for all the commodities (oil, copper, silver, zinc, nickel, etc.) that are traditionally exported by developing nations. So developing nations have been able to bring forward repayment of their debts, further reducing IMF resources. In April 2008 it was forced to announce the biggest shake-up of its funding since it first came into existence: it would cut 15 percent of its staff and – subject to US Congressional approval and legislation in some of its member nations – sell one-eighth of its gold reserve. The IMF has been traumatized both organizationally and ideologically.

Higher prices for raw materials and especially foodstuffs are likely to continue because rapid economic growth in China, India and elsewhere has created burgeoning demand that did not exist before, when the balance of trade systematically favored rich nations. The US has seen its net foreign asset position fall, whereas Japan, emerging Asia and oil-exporting nations have become far more powerful over the past decade and have become creditors to the US. As US deficits mount, with imports far greater than exports, the value of the dollar has declined, falling by 28 percent against the euro between 2001 and 2005.

The IMF and World Bank were also severely chastened by the 1997–2000 financial meltdowns in East Asia, Russia, and elsewhere. Many of their leaders lost faith in the anarchic premises, inherited from classical laissez-faire economic thought, which had guided their policy advice until then. Intellectually, both institutions are now far more defensive and concede that the premises that led to their creation in 1944 are hardly relevant to the way the real world now operates. Our "knowledge of economic growth is extremely incomplete," many in the IMF now admit, and it now needs "more humility." The IMF concedes that the international economy has been transformed dramatically and, as Stephen Roach of bankers Morgan Stanley has warned, the world "has done little to prepare itself for what could well be the next crisis."[3]

The nature of the global financial system has changed radically in ways that have nothing to do with virtuous national economic policies that follow IMF advice. The investment managers of private equity funds and major banks have displaced national banks and international bodies such as the IMF. In many investment banks, buccaneering traders have taken over from more cautious and traditional bankers and owners. Buying and selling shares, bonds, and derivatives now generate higher profits, and taking far greater risks is now the rule among what was once a fairly conservative branch of finance.

Profits, Real or Not

Such traders are rewarded on the basis of profits, fictitious or real, and routinely bet with house money. Low interest rates, and banks eager to lend money to hedge funds and firms that arrange mergers and acquisitions, have given such traders and others in the US, Japan and elsewhere a mandate to play financial games, including making dubious mergers that would once have been deemed foolhardy. In some cases, leveraged recapitalizations allow the traders to pay themselves enormous fees and dividends immediately, by adding to a company's debt burden. What happens later is someone else's problem.

Since the beginning of 2006 investment banks have vastly expanded their loans to leveraged buy-outs, pushing commercial banks out of a market they once dominated. To win a greater share of the market, they are making riskier deals and increasing the likelihood of defaults among highly leveraged firms – "living dangerously" as the head of Standard & Poor's bank loan ratings section put it. "Observers are predicting a sharp increase in defaults among highly leveraged companies," the *Financial Times* noted in July 2006.[4]

But there are fewer legal clauses to protect investors, so lenders are less likely than ever to compel mismanaged firms to default. Hedge funds, aware that their bets are more and more risky, are making it much more difficult to withdraw the money with which they play. Traders have "reintermediated" themselves between traditional borrowers (national and individual) and markets, further deregulating the world financial structure and making it far more susceptible to crises. They seek to generate high investment returns and take mounting risks to do so.

In March 2006 the IMF released Garry J. Schinasi's well-documented book *Safeguarding Financial Stability*, giving it unusual prominence.[5] The book is alarming, revealing and documenting as it does the IMF's deep anxieties in disturbing detail. Deregulation and liberalization, which the IMF and proponents of the Washington consensus have advocated for decades, have become a nightmare: they have created "tremendous private and social benefits" but also hold "the potential for fragility, instability, systemic risk, and adverse economic consequences."[6]

Schinasi concludes that the irrational development of global finance, combined with deregulation and liberalization, has "created scope for financial innovation and enhanced the mobility of risks." Schinasi and the IMF advocate a radical new framework to monitor and prevent the problems that are now enabled to emerge, but any success "may have as much to do with good luck" as with policy design and market surveillance. Leaving the future to luck is not at all what economics originally promised.

Even more alarming is a study, also publicized by the IMF and produced at the same time by establishment specialists, analyzing the problems that deregulation of the world financial structure has created. The authors believe that deregulation has caused "national financial systems [to] become increasingly vulnerable to increased systemic risk and to a growing number of financial crises."[7] The IMF shares the growing consensus among conservative banking experts that the world financial structure has now become far more precarious.

As the financial meltdown of Argentina in 1998 proved, countries that do not succumb to IMF and banker pressures can play on divisions within the IMF membership to avoid many, though not all, foreign demands. About $140 billion in sovereign bonds to private creditors and the IMF were at stake in Argentina, terminating in 2001 with the largest national default in history. Banks in the 1990s had been eager to lend Argentina money and they ultimately paid for their eagerness.

When Prices Soared

Since then, however, commodity prices have soared. The growth rate of developing nations in 2004 and 2005 was more than double that of high-income nations. They have increased, on the whole, even further in the period after 2006. As early as 2003 developing countries were already the source of 37 percent of the foreign direct investment in other developing nations. China accounts for much of this growth, which means that the IMF and rich bankers of New York, Tokyo, and London have far less leverage than before. After the financial crises in the developing world in the late 1990s, bankers resolved that they would be more cautious in the future, yet their current exposure to emerging market stocks and bonds is as great as ever because of far higher yields in Zambia or the Philippines, and excess cash. "The love affair is back on," said a bank trader.[8]

Growing complexity in the world economy and the endless negotiations of the World Trade Organization have failed to overcome the subsidies and protectionism that have thwarted a global free trade agreement and an end to the threat of trade wars. The potential for greater instability and danger for the rich now exists in the entire world economy.

The emerging global financial problem is proving inextricably tangled, with a fast-rising US fiscal and trade deficit. Since George Bush took presidential office in the US in 2001 he has added more than $3 trillion to federal borrowing limits, which are now almost $9 trillion. As long as there is a continued devaluation of the US dollar, banks and financiers will seek to guard their money and risky financial adventures will appear worthwhile. This is the context, but Washington had advocated greater financial deregulation long before the dollar weakened.

There are now at least 10,000 hedge funds, of which 8,000 are registered in the Cayman Islands. However, the 400 funds with $1 billion or more under management do 80 percent of the business. They cannot be regulated. They have over $1.5 trillion in assets and the daily global derivatives turnover is almost $6 trillion (equal to half the US gross domestic product). With the economic climate euphoric over the past five years, most funds have won, although some have lost. In the year ending August 2006, nearly 1,900 were created and 575 were liquidated. Standard & Poor would like to rank their credit-worthiness, but has yet to do so: bigger funds claim to use computer models to make trades, and three of the ten biggest claim they make purely quantitative decisions.

One of the most serious post-1945 financial threats to the global economy, the failure of the Long-Term Capital Management (LTCM) in 1998, involved a firm renowned for its mathematical trading techniques devised by two Nobel Prize laureates, Myron Scholes and Robert Merton.[9] The combined efforts of Washington and Wall Street prevented a disaster with LTCM, but the hedge funds are now much too big to be saved easily. In effect, hedge funds, which are extremely competitive, gamble and take great chances; they are attracted to credit derivatives and many similar devices invented with the promise of making money.[10] The credit derivative market was almost nonexistent in 2001, grew slowly until 2004 and then went into the stratosphere, reaching $26 trillion by June 2006. Many other financial instruments are now being invented, and markets for credit derivative futures, credit default swaps and binary options are in the offing.[11]

What are credit derivatives? The *Financial Times*' chief capital markets writer, Gillian Tett, tried to find out, but failed. The legend goes that around a decade ago bankers from JPMorgan were in Boca Raton, Florida, drinking and throwing each other into the swimming pool, when they came up with the notion of a new financial instrument that was too complex to be copied easily (since financial ideas cannot be copyrighted) and sure to make them money. Tett was critical of the potential of credit derivatives for causing a chain reaction of losses that could engulf the hedge funds that have jumped into this market. Bankers have become "ultra-creative in their efforts to slice, dice and redistribute risk, at this time of easy liquidity," she concluded. The *Financial Times* has in recent months run a series on financial wizardry which has been frankly skeptical of the means and ends of these innovations.[12]

One of the gurus of finance, Avinash Persaud, concluded that low interest rates have led investors to use borrowed money to play the markets, and "a painful deleveraging is as inevitable as night follows day ... the only question is its timing." There is no way that hedge funds, which have become intricate in their arrangements to seek safety, can avoid a reckoning, and they will be "forced to sell their most liquid investments." "I will not bet on that happy outcome," Gillian Tett concluded in her survey of belated attempts to redeem the hedge funds from their own follies.[13]

Warren Buffett, Forbes-listed as the second richest person in the world, has called credit derivatives "financial weapons

of mass destruction." Nominally they are insurance against
defaults, but they encourage greater gambles and credit
expansion, which are moral hazards. Enron used them
extensively; they were a secret of Enron's success and also of
its eventual bankruptcy with $100 billion losses.[14] They are
not monitored in any real sense, and experts have called them
"maddeningly opaque." Many innovative financial products,
according to a finance director, only "exist in cyberspace,"
often as tax dodges for the ultra-rich.[15]

Banks do not understand the chain of exposure and who
owns what: senior financial regulators and bankers now
admit this. Hedge funds claim to be honest, but those who
guide them are compensated for the profits they make, which
means taking risks. There are thousands of hedge funds and
many collect inside information. This is technically illegal
but it happens anyway.

Growing Danger

There is now a consensus that all this has created growing
financial dangers. We can put aside the persistence of
unbalanced national budgets based on spending increases
or tax cuts for the wealthy, and the world's volatile stock
and commodity markets which caused hedge funds to show
far lower returns in May 2006 than they have the past
year. Hedge funds still make plenty of profit but they are
increasingly dangerous.

It is too soon to estimate the ultimate impact of the recent
and widely publicized loss by Amaranth Advisors hedge fund
of more than $6 billion, representing over 60 percent of its
assets, within a single week.[16] Amaranth collaborated closely
with Morgan Stanley, Goldman Sachs and other important
investment houses, which explains why its losses caused such

a stir. The overall problems are structural, and include the greatly varying ratios between corporate debt loads and core earnings, which have grown substantially from four to six times over the past year because there are fewer legal clauses to protect investors from loss. They also keep companies from going bankrupt when they should. As long as interest rates have been low, leveraged loans have been the solution. Because of hedge funds and other financial instruments, there is now a market for incompetent and debt-ridden firms.[17] When the Ford Motor Company announced in September that it was losing over $7 billion annually, its bonds actually shot up 20 percent. The rules once associated with capitalism, such as probity and profit, no longer hold.

The problems inherent in speed and complexity are diverse and can be almost surreal. Credit derivatives are precarious enough, but in May the International Swaps and Derivatives Association revealed that one in every five deals, many of them involving billions of dollars, had major errors. As the volume of trade increased, so did the errors. They doubled after 2004. More than 90 percent of all deals in the US were not properly recorded, but put down only on paper and often just scraps at that.

In 2004 Alan Greenspan, then chairman of the US Federal Reserve, admitted to being "frankly shocked" by this situation. Efforts to remedy the mess only began in June and are far from resolving a major and accumulated problem involving stupendous sums. More importantly, deregulation and financial innovation have led to forms of crucial data that cannot be collected and quantified, leaving both bankers and governments in the dark about reality. We may or may not live in a new era of finance, but we certainly are flying blindfolded.

On April 24, Stephen Roach, Morgan Stanley's chief economist, wrote that a major financial crisis seemed imminent and that the global institutions that could forestall it, including the IMF, the World Bank and other mechanisms of the international financial architecture, were utterly inadequate.[18] Hong Kong's chief secretary deplored the hedge funds' risks and dangers in June, and at the same time the IMF's iconoclastic chief economist, Raghuram Rajan, warned that funds' compensation structures encouraged those in charge to take risks, endangering the whole financial system. Soon after, Roach was even more pessimistic: "a certain sense of anarchy" dominated academic and political communities "unable to explain the way the new world is working."[19] In its place, mystery prevailed. By September the IMF predicted that the risk of a severe slowdown in the global economy was greater than at any time since 2001, mainly because of the sharp decline in housing markets in the US and much of Western Europe; it also included the decline in US labor's real income and insufficient consumer purchasing power.[20] Even if the current level of prosperity endures through next year, and all these people are proved wrong, the transformation of the global financial system will sooner or later lead to dire results.

Reality is Out of Control

Reality is out of control. The entire global financial structure is becoming uncontrollable in crucial ways that its nominal leaders never expected, and instability is its hallmark. The scope and operation of international financial markets, their "architecture," as establishment experts describe it, has evolved haphazardly and its regulation is inefficient – indeed, almost nonexistent.[21]

Financial deregulation has produced a monster, and resolving the many problems that have emerged is scarcely possible for those who deplore controls on making money. The annual report of the Bank for International Settlements (BIS), released in June 2006, discusses these problems and the triumph of predatory economic behavior and trends "difficult to rationalize." The sharks have outflanked more conservative bankers. "Given the complexity of the situation and the limits of our knowledge, it is extremely difficult to predict how all this might unfold."[22] The BIS does not want its fears to cause panic, and circumstances compel it to remain on the side of those who are not alarmist. But it now concedes that a big crash in the markets is a possibility, and sees "several market-specific reasons for a concern about a degree of disorder."

We are "currently not in a situation" where a meltdown is likely to occur, but "expecting the best but planning for the worst" is still prudent. The BIS admits that, for a decade, global economic trends and financial imbalances have created worsening dangers, and "understanding how we got to where we are is crucial in choosing policies to reduce current risks."[23] The BIS is very worried.

Given such profound and widespread pessimism, vultures from investment houses and banks have begun to position themselves to profit from imminent business distress, a crisis they see as a matter of timing rather than principle. There is now a growing consensus among financial analysts that defaults will increase substantially in the near future. Because there is money to be made in the field, there is now great demand on Wall Street for experts in distressed debt and in restructuring companies in or near bankruptcy.

THE PREDICTED FINANCIAL STORM HAS ARRIVED
(ZNet, August 29, 2007)

Contradictions now wrack the world's financial system, and a growing consensus exists between those who endorse it and those who argue that the status quo is both crisis-prone and immoral. If we are to believe the institutions and personalities who have been in the forefront of the defense of capitalism, we are now on the verge of a serious crisis – or if not now, then in the near future.

The IMF, the Bank for International Settlements, the British Financial Services Authority, the *Financial Times*, and innumerable other mainstream commentators, were increasingly worried and publicly warned against many of the financial innovations that have now imploded. Very conservative individuals and institutions predicted the upheaval in global finances we are today experiencing.

The IMF has taken the lead in criticizing the new international financial structure, and over the past three years it has published numerous detailed reasons as to why that structure has become so dangerous to the world's economic stability. Events have confirmed its prognosis that complexity and lack of transparency, the obscurity of risks and universal uncertainty, especially regarding collateralized debt and loan obligations, would cause a flight to security that will dry up much of the liquidity of banking. As a *Financial Times* columnist put it, "financial innovation itself is the problem." The ultra-creative system is seizing up because no one understands where risks are located or how it works. It began to do so in the summer of 2007 and fixing it soon is not very likely.

It is impossible to measure the extent of the losses. The final results of this deluge have yet to be calculated. Even many of the players who have stakes in the countless arcane investment instruments are utterly ignorant. And the sums at risk are enormous.

We need only state a few of the many measures to give us a rough estimate: The present crisis began with sub-prime mortgage loans in the US, which were valued at over $1.3 trillion at the beginning of 2007 but are, for all practical purposes, worth far, far less today. We can ignore the impact of this crisis on US house prices, but some projections of the likely extent of that impact suggest a further 10 percent decline – another trillion dollars or so. Indirectly, of course, the mortgage crisis has also brought many millions of people into direct contact with problems in the larger financial world, and they will get badly hurt. What the sub-prime market did do was unleash a far greater maelstrom involving banks in Germany, France, Asia, and throughout the world, calling into question much of the world financial system as it has developed over the past decade.

Investment banks hold about $300 billion in private equity debts they had planned to place, mainly in leveraged buy-outs. They will be forced to sell these debts at discounts or keep them on their balance sheets – either way they will lose. The near failure of the German Sachsen LB bank, which had to be saved from bankruptcy with 17.3 billion euros in credit, revealed that European banks hold over half a trillion dollars in so-called asset-backed commercial paper, much of it in the US and sub-prime mortgages. The failure in America caused Europe too to face a crisis. The problem is scarcely isolated.

The major victims of this upheaval are the hedge funds. There are about 10,000 such funds and, all told, they take chances on everything. Some hedge funds provided companies with capital and successfully competed with commercial banks because they took much greater risks. A substantial proportion are simply gamblers; some even bet on the weather. Many look to their computers and mathematical models to guide their investments, and these funds have lost the most money, but those based on other strategies also lost during August 2007. The spectacular failure in 1998 of the Long-Term Capital Management hedge fund was also due to its reliance on ingenious mathematical propositions, yet no one learned any lessons from it, proving that appeals to reason as well as experience fall on deaf ears where there is money to be made.

Some gained during the August crisis but still more lost, and in the aggregate the hedge funds lost a great deal – their allure of rapid riches gone. There have been some spectacular bankruptcies and bailouts, including some of the biggest investment firms. Investors who got cold feet found that withdrawing money from hedge funds was nigh on impossible. The real worth of their holdings is hotly contested, and valuations vary wildly. In effect, there is no way to appraise them realistically – they all depend largely on what people want to believe and will take.

We are at an end of an era, living through the worst financial panic in many decades, entering a period of global financial instability and the decline of the United States' hegemony. It is impossible to speculate how long today's turmoil will last, but there now exists an uncertainty and lack of confidence unparalleled since the 1930s, and this ignorance and fear is itself a crucial factor. The moment of reckoning for bankers and bosses has arrived. What is very clear is that losses are massive and the entire developed world is now experiencing the worst economic crisis since 1945, one in which troubles in one nation compound those in others.

All central banks are wracked by dilemmas. They have neither the resources nor the knowledge, including legal powers, to remedy the present maelstrom. Although there is clamor from financiers and assorted operators to bail them out, the Federal Reserve must also weigh the consequences of its moves, above all for inflation. Then there is the question of "moral hazard." Is it the Federal Reserve's responsibility to save financial adventurers from their own follies? Throughout August, the American and European central banks plunged about a half-trillion dollars into the banking system in an attempt to unfreeze blocked credit and loans that followed the sub-prime crisis – an event which triggered a "flight to safety" which in turn greatly reduced the banks' willingness to loan. In effect, the Federal Reserve relied on the banks to restore confidence in the financial system, subsidizing their efforts.

The central banks' efforts succeeded only very partially and, in the aggregate, they failed: banks and investors now seek security rather than risk, and they will sit on their money. The Federal Reserve privately acknowledges its inability to cope with an inordinately complex financial structure. European central bankers are in exactly the same dilemma: they simply don't know what to do.

But this scarcely touches the real problem, which is structural and impinges wholly on the way the world financial structure has evolved over the past two decades. As in the past, there is a critical split between the banking and finance world and each has political leverage along with clashing interests. More important, central banks were not designed to cope with today's realities and have neither the legal powers nor the knowledge to control them.

It is not only Leftists who are naive, but so too those conservatives who think they can speak truth to power and change the course of events. Neither existing international institutions – of which the IMF is the most important – nor well-intentioned advice will change this situation.

2
The Contours of Recent American Foreign Policy

War, from preparation for it through to its aftermath, has defined both the essential nature of the major capitalist nations and their relative power since at least 1914. War became the major catalyst of change for revolutionary movements in Russia, China, and Vietnam. While wars also created reactionary and fascistic parties, particularly in the case of Italy and Germany, in the longer run they brought about domestic social changes of far-reaching magnitude. The Bolshevik Revolution was the preeminent example of this ironic symbiosis of war and revolution.

Wars not only created social disorder within nations, producing revolutions on the Right and Left, they also reduced the ability of capitalist states to compete economically with each other. To a significant degree, the United States' economic supremacy up to the Vietnam War was based on the economic consequences of the two World Wars for Europe. Europe made war while America produced war goods for them until it was ready to enter into war later on its own terms. After 1964, the pattern was reversed, as the US weakened itself through war while the Europeans and Japanese made consumer goods and prospered.

The policy choices made by the US and most other nations always depended on the health – or lack of it – of the economy. Economic necessities restrict the options policymakers can consider. What a nation can afford is crucial in determining what it can do in the long run. The nature of a power structure – which individuals and classes have the most influence – in turn shapes the range of policies that decision-makers are likely to select from. The political role of the corporations with the most to gain in a nation has always been greatly disproportionate to their numbers. They have created a larger consensus among those who matter most in politics. They have provided, to a remarkable degree, the personnel and expertise essential for the evaluation and direction of foreign policy. All this may seem perfectly self-evident but it is worth reminding ourselves that – among other things but often principally – foreign policies reflect the nature of interested parties, which may be corporate (a constituency itself often very divided), or ethnic (constituencies no less divided by their conceptions of how best the US should relate to situations), or include other interest groups of every shape and variety.

Historically, the main capitalist nations maintained a consensus against all social revolutions in the Third World. This consensus, however, eroded and fell apart as national trade interests came to into play over rivalries for oil and critical raw materials, and as the desire to integrate ex-colonial nations (as artificial as many were) into spheres of influence became more pressing. As a result, there was an escalating power conflict between Western Europe, the United States, Japan, and, more recently, China. The war in Vietnam made the new assertiveness and real power of other nations possible, as the inflation- and deficit-ridden American economy saw the dollar weakened and the gold standard abandoned under Lyndon Johnson.

All that the US made certain was uncertainty itself, leading to a future marked by frequent crises in financial and foreign policy areas, depending on the interests involved. All of this seems self-evident, but is apparently not so to those who rule nations, largely because the interests at stake are always different and there are simply too many nuances to master.

Radical critics cannot draw up a timetable or predict the exact magnitude of future crises because their analytic perceptions are deficient, having lost their appeal and sounding increasingly hollow. But those who rule our political and economic institutions have the problem of resolving the challenges they inherit, and their past incapacity to do so without creating turmoil for some constituency of American society – generally the poor and underprivileged – bequeaths a dismal future to those who are likely to lose the most.

The problem of running a vast foreign and military policy, not just for the United States but also for other nations, is that all decisions on vital questions are filtered through the prism of ambition. Since men and women who aspire to attain influence and power very often give advice with a view to advancing their own careers, they are generally anything but objective assessors of options. Decisions are made to attain success; choices are rarely made with an eye on the facts. The war in Iraq was an example of this. In April 2008 the National Defense University report on the Iraq War, which called it "a major debacle," was written by men who had originally fully supported the war in order to advance their careers, but who later realized the necessity of turning against it for the political expediency of keeping Congressional money flowing. Decisions, in short, ought to be arrived at without reference to the demands of the bureaucratic system or the calculations of individuals as to how a given decision will affect their personal future. But the current decision-making system is tainted. Errors may be made innocently, as they frequently are, by misjudging facts or being ignorant of vital information, but the system also has the problem of ambitious people. All rational expectation theories, including the schematic notions of Max Weber and the like in sociology, make very similar errors.

All of Bush's major policies, especially his wars in Afghanistan and Iraq and the grandiose neoconservative agenda to make the US the dominant world power, have failed, leaving a legacy of fear and hatred in the Middle East and much of the rest of the world, while making an enemy of Russia and weakening America's traditional alliances. These policies also made Bush the most unpopular president in American history. Rather than vindicate the Pentagon's power and succeed in extirpating terrorist evils, the wars in Afghanistan and Iraq have shown yet again that the US cannot impose its will on nations determined to resist it. The wars have also gravely destabilized the Muslim world, Pakistan, and the entire South Asia region, making nuclear proliferation a greater danger than ever. Like America's attempt to destroy the Vietnamese communists, the US attack on Saddam Hussein's regime has again revealed the limits of its power. Worse yet, in the Middle East Bush's war in Iraq has – as his father feared it would – left Iran as the dominant power in the region and transformed the balance of power in favor of a nation the US chose to make its enemy. Contradictions and disasters are the leitmotif of virtually everything the second George Bush did, but there is also a crucial continuity between his own Administration and that of his father from 1989 through 1992.

Following the collapse of the Soviet Union in August 1991 the US lacked an identifiable enemy. Now that the Cold War adversary was gone, the fear of communism had to be replaced by another mobilizing anxiety. President George H.W. Bush and most of his advisers wished to see the USSR survive in some form. "We have an interest in the stability of the Soviet Union," Brent Scowcroft, the president's National Security Adviser, told Bush. "Historical enemies would be less constrained by the bipolar Superpower alignments," the US Joint Chiefs of Staff stated in 1991. Communism had been dangerous but predictable, and the danger now was "international deregulation."[1] What was essential was a new doctrine to replace fear of communism, one that would keep Congress and the American public ready to spend inordinate sums to sustain the US military as the strongest on earth.

The first President Bush assigned this definitional problem to his Secretary of Defense, Dick Cheney, who later became vice-president under his son. Cheney published a grandiose picture of a dominant American military power so great and omnipotent – and expensive – globally that no nation could rival it. The policy was vague as to which nation or enemy it was directed against, but it included the abandonment of the doctrine of nuclear deterrence and a commitment to the use of nuclear weapons against lesser threats: weapons of mass destruction, menaces of an indefinable nature. It was later to form the basis of the neoconservative vision under the second Bush Administration. It was never repudiated, in fact was essentially continued, by the Clinton Administration. Indeed, it has not been repudiated by anyone, whether Republicans or Democrats, even to this day. When parts of Cheney's vision were published in 1993 the Japanese and the Germans were already deemed to be, once again, potential challengers to American power. After the Gulf War of 1990, Iraq was considered an enemy but also strategically important to the US simply because Saddam Hussein – once a US ally and the recipient of billions of dollars of aid – effectively contained Iranian power. Who was the enemy? If this has remained unclear, it is today US policy that it is prepared to use nuclear weapons against non-nuclear threats – abandoning deterrence for something far more amorphous in terms of the practical consequences.

The continuity between the reigns of the two Presidents Bush is clear enough, as is the fact that the use of nuclear weapons to respond to non-nuclear threats, and the abandonment of deterrence, was also the policy of the Clinton Administration. They in turn were all part of a confrontation with the world that began under President Harry Truman. The rise of Cheney was scarcely an accident: he became vice-president to fulfill a consummately ambitious doctrine committed to dangers, and although the senior Bush later regretted the way the policy was interpreted, Cheney was also the author of what has proved the most grandiose of all efforts: articulating a mobilizing doctrine to replace the fear of communism with an indefinable enemy and threat that will justify the Pentagon's immense and growing budget.

The United States' problem is compounded today by the deepening disparity between its military doctrines and reality, and by much else. When we discuss US foreign policy we must differentiate between the ideology and the motives that have guided it in the Western Hemisphere, from as early as 1823 when the Monroe Doctrine excluded the colonial European powers from any further expansion and left the entire region to the US, which even then was eyeing great parts of Mexico and the Spanish empire for itself. (Even today, only 82 percent of all Americans speak English. Most of the others speak Spanish.) The US interventions that came much later in Europe were ad hoc responses to the crises between European nations that emerged from the breakup of colonialism, or to fears of communism – sometimes real but often fictional and convenient. Many of these responses were unpredictable and involved everything from a need to ensure the "credibility" of military power – as in Vietnam – to sheer ideological fixation and a belief that firepower would solve political challenges quickly, as in the case of the present war in Iraq. Crises in the Western Hemisphere, like those that emerged elsewhere since 1947, may also have involved unpredictability, but the US role in the West has often, perhaps always, possessed a crucial geopolitical dimension that rarely, perhaps never, existed in Asia or the Middle East. Economically and strategically one must always look at crises in the Western Hemisphere through a prism that is much older – and more vital to the United States' real interests. Less than a fifth of its petroleum today comes from the entire Persian Gulf, where it is fighting what has become a major war. Wars in the Eastern Hemisphere take the US away from its own interest and history.

But the United States seeks and finds other problems. The Korean War first revealed America's inability to match a fighting and technological capacity directed against Soviet and centralized or urban targets – for which its atomic bombs and mobile armor were best suited – and the decentralized battlefields which it confronted in Korea and Vietnam, and confronts today in Iraq, to mention only the best known. The Vietnam War was a futile, expensive, and protracted effort to use high mobility and airpower – helicopters and B52s – to fight a jungle-based, highly decentralized guerilla army. There was even then growing doctrinal confusion, compounded by the proliferation of nuclear weapons, and today the US suffers an even more acute doctrinal crisis. Its wars in Afghanistan and Iraq have been costly beyond imagination, will endure long after those who began them leave Washington, and yet will end in failure. There is a rationale for higher Defense spending because it sustains arms builders who have tremendous power in Washington, but their promises of success have proven a chimera. Indeed, military contractors often simply want to sell arms, not use them. Some of them, indeed, may even be against the wars in which their products are employed.

The disparity between military technology and reality (which I discuss in greater detail in Chapter 7) has also affected America's allies, such as Israel. Today this gap between what its military arm can do and political reality poses an even graver problem for America than did the wars in Korea and Vietnam. The American military cannot organize sufficiently well for its missions because they are potentially limitless – taking in Asia, South and Central America, Eastern Europe and Russia, and the entire world. It was not able to fight successfully in either Korea or Vietnam, and its foreign and military policies are often an adventure. The US never fought a communist nation in Eastern Europe though it prepared to do so. It succeeds, if at all, only in very small nations where its proxies are venal and corrupt. But communist Cuba has existed since 1959!

The problem for the United States is that communism for practical purposes has virtually ceased to exist – what passes as communism in China, Vietnam, or North Korea is increasingly no more than a pretentious fraud. They are de facto capitalist nations or Confucian tyrannies. The US does not know who its enemies are and has the military muscle, and technology, designed to fight only communism.

So long as communism was the enemy a US-led alliance could be bound together by a unifying theme. When fear of communism disappeared, more particular interests took over and nations began finding their own way while distancing themselves from American leadership. The situation since 1991 has become far more complicated – a fact America's leaders in Washington realized as soon as the USSR collapsed. The world has become far more unstable and unpredictable and the so-called "globalization" of the world economy has made it more rather than less precarious.

Now nations have power without ideology in the true sense of that term, leaving the US confused as never before. The ideological era is over, for capitalists as well as those descended from the Marxist tradition. "Terrorism" is no less confusing. Is it Islamic jihadist, secular nationalist, or what? The US's efforts against "terrorism" are often counterproductive, as in Afghanistan and Somalia, leaving its enemies stronger than ever. American foreign policy is in crisis because parts of the world are now in transition, emerging from 70 years of Bolshevism into an amorphous political landscape in which a coherent, identifiable adversary can no longer be found.

Worse yet for the United States, its preoccupation with one nation or region – Vietnam and Iraq are perfect examples – means that it lacks the resources to destroy often far more serious opposition elsewhere. The US adventure in Vietnam meant that Castro's Cuba had the time and space to consolidate – such that a hostile regime calling itself communist still exists only 90 miles from the US. The Afghan and Iraq wars have likewise allowed a slew of Leftist regimes in South America virtual freedom to consolidate, even though ultimately the Western Hemisphere is far more important to the US, strategically at least, than are the wars it loses elsewhere. In a word, the US squanders its vast but ultimately limited resources capriciously. It cannot manage its power rationally.

Above all, its martial adventures abroad cost far more than the US can now afford. As detailed in the previous chapter, now is an inauspicious moment to be an imperial power: the prices of the commodities the US imports are rising, its current account deficit is worsening, the value of the dollar is falling, while the wars in Afghanistan and Iraq have become the most expensive in American history. The US began to fight in Afghanistan in October 2001, but has failed to capture Osama bin Laden, thought to be the man behind the terrorist attacks on America on September 11 which killed nearly 3000 people. Meanwhile, the Taliban is becoming stronger and the conflict has spread into northern Pakistan, destabilizing that nation's politics. Since Pakistan possesses nuclear weapons, Washington feels there is a grave risk that Muslim extremists will acquire such a weapon and then be capable of destroying an American city, or all of Israel.

Everything is going wrong for the United States in terms of its power position globally. Russia – now rich from selling gas and oil, while spending on its military less than a fifth of the US expenditure in 2006 – is still the US's equal in terms of nuclear weapons, and outflanks the US in Central Asia, the Middle East, and much of the Islamic world. It sells sophisticated arms to many nations, has economic agreements with Arab and Muslim countries, and has become a growing obstacle to America's influence and power. Russia is just as much a danger to the US as when Stalin ruled. Nuclear proliferation is now a grave problem, with an unpredictable but growing number of nations equipped with nuclear bombs and terrorists more and more likely to get hold of them. As for chemical and biological weapons, the US never even caught its anthrax killer soon after the September 11 attack. At the same time, the Bush Administration's strategy on Iran is being undermined by rising oil and gas prices, which also have the effect of making the successors to the Soviet system even richer. There is a fatal, impossible contradiction between US goals – to eliminate the present Teheran regime and contain Russian power – and rising petroleum prices. American policy on Russia is a shambles.

In crucial ways, the basic approach and limits of US foreign policy are hardly unusual. The US suffers from the kind of problems that have affected many nations over the past centuries. The only difference is that the US had, and to a great degree still has, power even while undergoing a transition away from the omnipotence it enjoyed after 1945. That alone is its distinction. The existing system – whether American or not – has the fundamental problem that it cannot be run according to rational criteria, and like Marxism it has no "laws." In every nation, in every branch of life – military, political, cultural – there are a sufficient number of adventurers, opportunists, egomaniacs, psychotics, or destructive individuals who create or accept disorder. In the case of the US, James V. Forrestal, the first Secretary of Defense, jumped out of the window of a naval hospital – to which he was confined for paranoia – in May 1949, allegedly because he believed war with the USSR was imminent. Other types – sheer opportunists such as the neoconservatives crucial in the Bush Administration – wish to accumulate power alone. Ideologies are very often merely a disguise for ambition. This limit, again, exists everywhere, not just the United States, and regardless of whether the party in power calls itself "socialist," "capitalist," or whatever.

Cynicism is prevalent, and often the only motive of political behavior. We can see it in Russia or Great Britain today. And this is the case not simply with respect to foreign policy, but in relation to every aspect of existing society.

People, whether theorists, administrators, or whatever, cannot regulate or predict systems run by ambitious individuals, and they frequently cannot regulate systems run by perfectly sincere people either – it is simply far too difficult. There is often an immense disparity between what politicians – whatever they call themselves and no matter which nation they belong to – do and what they say. What they do, not what they say, is crucial, because in countless places they have often betrayed their followers.

MECHANISTIC DESTRUCTION:
AMERICAN FOREIGN POLICY AT POINT ZERO
(Antiwar.com, August 7, 2007)

The United States has rarely lost a conventional military battle since at least 1950. But nor has it, at the same time, ever won a war. It has successfully overthrown governments through intervention or subversion, but the political results of all its efforts, as in Afghanistan in the 1980s and Iran in 1953, have often made its subsequent geopolitical position far more tenuous. In short, in international affairs it blunders very badly and has made an already highly unstable world far more precarious than it otherwise would be had the US refrained from interfering in global affairs. No less important, Americans would be far better off as a result. Because, to repeat the critical point, the US has failed to attain victory in any of the wars it has fought since Korea. Its adversaries learned as long ago as the Korean War that a decentralized conflict would stymie America's overwhelming firepower, which was designed for concentrated armies, and provide a successful antidote to the use of massive and expensive technology.

All this is very well known. The real issue is why the US makes the identical mistakes over and over again and never learns from its errors. At the present time it is losing two wars and creating a vast arc of profound strategic and political instability from the Mediterranean Sea to South Asia; it has resumed the arms race in Europe, and it is making an enemy of Russia when it could easily have been friendly. Wherever one turns, the Bush Administration has been at least as bad as any in two centuries of American history, perhaps even the worst. We now have an unprecedented disaster in the conduct of American power, both overseas and at home, in part because of the people who now rule – ambitious men and women who calculate only what is best for their careers – but also because the imperatives and inexorable logic of past policies and conventional wisdom have brought us to this critical juncture. All the old mistakes have been repeated; nothing has been learned from the past, and official myopia is persistent.

A large part of the United States' problem, whether Republicans or Democrats are in power, is that it believes it has the right and obligation to intervene everywhere, in whatever form it chooses, and that its interests are global. Interventionism, so the consensus among both Republicans and Democrats goes, is the price to be paid for its global interest and mission. In this regard, there was nothing unique about the second Bush Administration. This global pretension, which originated during the nineteenth century in the context of the Western Hemisphere and which Woodrow Wilson articulated, is simply not functional and has led the US into countless morasses, detrimental to its own interests but far worse for the countries in which it has interfered. The fact is that no nation has ever been able to assume such an international role, and those that have attempted to came to no good end. They exhausted their resources and passions and follies.

Political conflicts are not solved by military interventions, and that they are often incapable of being resolved by political or peaceful means either does not alter the fact that force is dysfunctional. This is more true today than ever with the spread of weapons technology. The US is not exempt from the realities that have guided international affairs for centuries. It has already lost the wars in Iraq and Afghanistan for the very same reasons it lost all of its earlier conflicts. It has the advantage in terms of manpower and firepower, as always, but these are ultimately irrelevant in the medium and long term. And such force was no more relevant in many contexts where the US was not involved – for example, France in Algeria or the Soviet Union in Afghanistan – and explains the outcome of many armed struggles over the past century regardless of who was involved in them, for they are usually decided by the socio-economic and political strength of the various sides. China after 1947 and Vietnam after 1972 are two examples, but scarcely the only ones. It is a transcendent truism of global politics that wars are determined more by socio-economic and political factors than by any other, and this was true long before the US attempted to regulate the world's affairs.

But Why?

But all this still begs the question as to why the US repeatedly makes the same drastic errors. Are there vested interests involved in preparing for war? Are illusions about US power based on such interests, or on ideologies – or both?

In part, the incredibly inflated US military budget is premised on the traditional assumption that owning complex, technologically advanced weapons gives America power, which is determined by arms in hand rather than by what happens in a nation politically and socially. In fact, the reverse is often the case, especially when enemies find the weaknesses in this sort of technology and exploit it, as they increasingly have done over the past decades. Then the cost of fighting wars becomes a liability, and maintaining America's incredibly expensive military machine becomes an immense weakness when the government has huge deficits or lacks the funds to repair its aging public infrastructure – a fact that was highlighted when the collapse of a bridge in Minneapolis in the summer of 2007 led to the striking revelation that 70,000 bridges in the US are rated structurally deficient.

The Vietnam War should have resolved the issue of the relevance of technology to America's military ambitions, but it did not. The US military only increased its technological base so that the war in Iraq, deploying roughly 140,000 soldiers, cost it about five times as much as the Vietnam War, where a maximum of 550,000 troops were deployed. The Iraq War ranks as the most expensive in the postwar period because it is based on high technology weapons. Even more dangerous yet, America's military is experiencing the same process of demoralization as occurred in Vietnam. A protracted war in Iraq is again wrecking the American army, which has been compelled to rely on soldiers serving multiple tours of duty. US officers now believe overwhelmingly that the army is overstretched, regardless of the technology so freely showered upon it.

The real question is: why has the US persisted with this technological folly?

In a critical sense, the Pentagon's penchant for military toys makes an ambitious and aggressive foreign policy essential. Without enemies and conflicts, real or potential, there would be no reason to spend money; a fact that often colored the Pentagon's definition of Soviet goals after 1947, despite the objections of senior CIA analysts. But the Defense Department, and the national security establishment in general, is immense, and all kinds of constituencies exist within it. There are procurement experts who draw up budgets and go after new equipment mindlessly, but also strategists who see the futility of more arms spending. Each does their own thing and they are often very different. These contradictions have always existed side by side.

But those who run the military establishment have technological illusions, which when translated into competing budget demands keep immense sums of money flowing to arms manufacturers and their minions. There is a very profound consensus between the two parties on arms spending, which began under the Truman-era Democrats a half-century ago and will not go away – no matter how neglected the bridges and infrastructure, the health services, and the like. Arms lobbies are not only very powerful in Washington; weapons manufacturers create crucial jobs in most states and military spending keeps the economy afloat. Weapons producers make money regardless of whether the Pentagon wins or loses its wars – and making money is their only objective. Many of them were horrified when it was proposed that their arms be used to expand the war in the Gulf region to include Iran. This is surely a key causal factor, even if it is far from being the sole explanation, of why the US repeatedly intervenes where it shouldn't.

It is close to impossible to determine the true power of the arms industry but it must be taken into account that the arms manufacturers have strategic lobbies in Washington, contribute heavily to politicians who need campaign funding, and gain financially whether America wins or loses its wars. The arms industry is scarcely the only factor in the foreign policy equation, but it is of undoubted importance.

Another explanation is ambitious politicians who will say and do whatever is required to stay in power or to gain it. This factor is by now so familiar that it scarcely requires repeating, but the cynical ways politicians treat polls and American public opinion is a crucial aspect of the issue. There are indeed problems with the public, but invariably it senses realities and seeks to impose constraints well before the politicians do so – who tend to use the public and then ignore it. The party out of office will cater to mass opinion but usually forgets it once it comes to power, as the recent highly ambiguous Democratic Party trajectory shows. This is usually the rule, but public opinion is an element that cannot be merely gainsaid, and as the Korean and Vietnam wars proved it can play a decisive role. An increasing majority of people in the US think the war in Iraq is not worth fighting, and while the public may be, and generally is, impotent or far too passive for its own good, it is far less brainwashed than the advocates of "manufactured consent" concede. In time, it responds to foreign policies that are too costly or clash with its other priorities, ensuring that what happens in the economy is vitally important, both for the public and also for decision-makers. George W. Bush eventually ranked as the most unpopular president in modern American history, with the war in Iraq and the economy being cited as the major reasons. How, when, or if the role of the public becomes more crucial, and an obstacle for those in power who prefer war to peace, is a matter of conjecture. Its influence is usually negligible and takes far too long to have an impact. Follies continue to be committed long after the public has condemned them. But that it eventually becomes critical is a fact of life which one cannot make too much of, or too little.

That Bush's policies have failed and are increasingly dangerous as a guide to action has been true for a long time and is more obvious as the years elapse. The present Administration encapsulates it, but the basic problem has existed for many decades. What the Bush coterie has effected is the culmination of a logic that is far older. It presides over a catastrophe that began many years ago.

Some of the most acute criticisms made of the gross over-simplifications guiding interventionist policies have come from within the military, particularly since the trauma of the Vietnam experience. My history of the Vietnam War was purchased by many military base libraries, and the military journals treated it in detail and very respectfully. The statement at the end of July 2007 by the new chairman of the Joint Chiefs of Staff, Admiral Michael G. Mullen, that no amount of troops in no amount of time will make much of a difference if Iraqi politics fails to change drastically, reflects a current of realism that has existed among military thinkers for some decades (whether the Admiral will act on his statement is another matter, and depends greatly on considerations outside of his control). Like the CIA, the military has acute strategic thinkers, and the monographs of the US Army's Strategic Studies Institute – to name one of many sources – are often very insightful and critical. Academics tend to be irrelevant and dull by comparison.

The problem, of course, is that few (if any) at the decisive level pay any attention to the critical ruminations consistently produced by the military and the CIA. There is no shortage of insight among US official analysts; the problem is that policy is rarely formulated with objective knowledge acting as a constraint. Ambitious people say what their superiors wish to hear, and rarely if ever contradict them. Iraq is but one example, for the entire mess there was predicted. But those in power simply ignore the military's critical insights, and the vast bulk of officers obey orders even though many of them know better. They have learned the hard way – through a level of experience that neocon intellectuals and scribblers utterly lack. Neoconservative ideology may have been exhausted, and many are becoming defensive, but there still are a few holding on to the original faith or impulse, and they remain crucial in the Republican Party.

We are at point zero in the application of American power in the world: the US cannot win its extremely expensive adventures in North Korea, Afghanistan, Iraq, and elsewhere, nor will it abstain from policies which increasingly lead to disasters for the nations in which it intervenes, and for itself as well. All the factors I have mentioned – the myopia regarding technology, the policy consensus that binds ambitious politicians and often makes public opinion irrelevant, the arms makers and their local interests, or the limits of rational input – have all combined to deliver us to this impasse. It is difficult not to be pessimistic when we allow – as we should – realism rather than illusions to guide our political assessments. But realism is the only way to avoid cynicism.

A RATIONAL PERSPECTIVE ON OUR PRESENT CRISES
(Revised preface for the German-language edition of
The Age of War, 2007)

It is understandable that intelligent people should be preoccupied with the crises reported in the daily press, but they are best comprehended in their historical context. That context, and the crucial causes and motives guiding American foreign policy since 1950, are key to understanding the often bewildering and multidimensional events since the year 2000. George W. Bush and his cronies have done incalculable damage and committed terrible follies, but it is a fundamental error to assume that Bush is somehow original and the genesis of our present crisis.

It is much riskier to focus on particulars as if they have no precedents or are not part of an older, longer historical pattern. Indeed, a major fault of many assessments of US actions abroad is precisely such a disregard for the circumstances that led to them and for their historical framework.

The world has changed with increasing speed over the last half-century, and there have been more wars and upheavals over the past decade than at any time since 1945. Given the weaponry now available, and the growing political and diplomatic instability that has accompanied the demise of communism, this is the most dangerous period in mankind's entire history. It is also the period of greatest changes in the balance of world forces, with not only the decentralization of powerful weapons but the reemergence of nationalist, ethnic, and religious factors. The breakup of the USSR was only partially the cause.

How global military, political, economic, and other variables interact is very often unpredictable, to which one must add the variables associated with domestic politics and public moods within crucial nations, of which the US is most important. World affairs are not only complex but also full of surprises – not only for us but also for those in Washington and elsewhere who aspire to control the destiny of humanity.

Contradictions and errors have characterized the policies and actions of all ambitious nations, leading to wars that are not only far bloodier and longer than anticipated but that also produce such unwanted political and social consequences as revolution, or its opposite, reaction. The emergence of communism and fascism, and the sequence of wars over the past century, was merely confirmation of the fact that, once the fighting begins, human values and institutions – all the forces that create social stability – go awry.

George W. Bush inherited conventional wisdom regarding the world mission and universal interests that guide American policies on the world scene. The same ambitions have often been shared by leaders of other powers who believed that wars served as effective, controllable instruments of national goals. What Bush did do, however, was intensify the most dangerous traits always inherent in American institutions and beliefs since 1945. He scarcely expected to get bogged down in the affairs of the Middle East, making Iran the strategically most important power in the entire region and reducing US influence and prestige there to the lowest point it has ever been. Still less did he imagine that America's war would rip apart the existing fragile political arrangements and boundaries so that the specter of civil war and bloodshed along sectarian and ethnic lines in the entire Middle East may last for decades to come. President John F. Kennedy and his successors had similarly expected that their involvement in Vietnam would be limited and short.

But once the shooting begins – and America's "credibility" is at stake – these zones of conflict become automatic priorities for the US. Moreover, what is crucial is that its pretensions and ambitions have often led the US to very different parts of the globe, where it frequently loses control over the military and political results of its many interventions. The world has always been very large and very complex, and is becoming more so. The US may eventually adjust to that reality. But it has refused to do so in the past as well as in the present.

Both Presidents George H.W. Bush and Bill Clinton radically altered the justifications for the United States' global foreign policy after communism disappeared. The second Bush claims there is "a decisive ideological struggle" against Islamic fundamentalism and "terrorism," and expected a quick victory in the 2003 Iraq War followed by the overthrow of the regimes in Iran and Syria. Fighting Islamic fundamentalism and terrorism is the main rationale for the wars the US is now waging in Afghanistan and Iraq, and it may yet be used to justify extending the fighting elsewhere. But Bush's predecessors concocted variations of these themes based on fear and anxiety in large part to justify massive military spending after the demise of the USSR; likewise "preemptive" interventions have provided a rationale for American foreign policy for many decades.

Yet while an alleged Islamic terrorist threat took communism's place throughout the 1990s, it did so in an often-contrived fashion that made exceptions to accommodate America's important alliances with Saudi Arabia, Pakistan, and other orthodox Muslim states. But Islam has existed for centuries, it has changed very little, and the US often utilized fundamentalist religion in Iran, Afghanistan, and elsewhere after 1950 as an antidote against godless communism. What was crucial was that the US needed a threat and an alleged danger in order to legitimize to its own population its global role and readiness to intervene everywhere. This justification causes it to spend almost as much on its military machine as the entire rest of the world combined.

The Middle East and South-Central Asia since 2001, at the very latest, have posed the leading crises facing the US and the world as a whole. These are conflicts with Islamic nations but they hardly existed when there were communist states to cope with. President Woodrow Wilson predicted in 1919 that if the peace made after the war were not just, "there will follow not mere conflict but cataclysm."[2] The reemergence of Islamic ideologies, the rise of secular nationalism in the region, Zionism and the seemingly intractable Arab–Jewish conflict, and much else besides, is a result, to a crucial extent, of the role of outside foreign intervention.

World War II was further vindication of Wilson's fears, and today we are experiencing the irrationality of the settlements in the Middle East that followed World War I. While these are conflicts which scarcely featured for Washington while communist states existed, they were latent and came to define the "enemy" after 1991 because it was essential to concoct fear. They were therefore convenient but also natural. The US needed a new enemy and Islamic nations that were once its friends became its foes.

Communism is all but dead but the world's sufferings have, if anything, increased with the disappearance of what was the justification for the Cold War. The immense resources that the US and mankind might have devoted to making peace and meeting rational human needs and desires have instead gone to preparing for and making war. Today we confront the indefinite prospect of war and human suffering on a vast scale. This has also been the case for at least the past half-century but now that military weaponry is far more destructive, and readily available to fundamentalist groups unafraid of death, the prospects for global peace are diminishing yet further.

THE DILEMMAS OF AMERICAN FOREIGN POLICY
(Revised version of a *L'Unita* interview published December 16, 2005; also partially based on the updated 2005 Italian edition of my 1994 book, *The Century of War*)

The dilemma the US has had for a half-century is that the priorities it needs to impose on its budget and policies have never guided its actual behavior and actions. It has always believed, as well it should, that Europe and its control would determine the future of world power. But it has fought in Korea, Vietnam, and now Afghanistan and Iraq – in the so-called "Third World" in general – where the stakes in terms of military power were much smaller even when these nations were economically and geopolitically important. Its priorities were specific, focused on particular nations, but they also set the United States the task of guiding or controlling the entire world – which has proven time and again to be far beyond American resources and power. In most of those places in the Third World where the US has massively and directly employed its power it has lost, and its military might has proven ineffective. Its local proxies have been corrupt and venal in most nations where it has relied upon them. The cost, both financially and in terms of the eventual alienation of the American public, has been monumental.

The Pentagon developed strategic airpower and nuclear weaponry with the USSR as the primary target, and equipped itself to fight a land war in Eastern Europe. Arms manufacturers much preferred this expensive approach, and they remain very powerful. But the Soviet enemy no longer exists. The US dilemma, and it betrays a fundamental contradiction, is that its expensive military machine is largely useless as an instrument of foreign policy. It lost the war in Vietnam, and while it managed to overthrow popular regimes in Brazil, Chile, and elsewhere in Latin America, its military power is useless in dealing with the effects of larger social and political problems – and Latin America, the Middle East, and East Asia are more independent of American control than ever.

Strategically also, the US is far worse off in the oil-rich Middle East because it has made every mistake possible. It supported Islamic fundamentalism against communism but also against secular nationalism; it supported Iraq against Iran in the 1980s; and it is now not only losing the war in Iraq militarily but also alienating most of its former friends in the region. Meanwhile Iran is emerging as the decisive power in the area.

The basic problem the world confronts today is American ambition, an ambition based on the illusion that its great military power allows it to define political and social trends everywhere it chooses to do so. When the USSR existed it was somewhat more inhibited because Soviet military power neutralized American military might and there was a partial equilibrium – a deterring balance of terror – in Europe. Moreover, the USSR always advised allies and nations in its orbit to move carefully so as not to provoke the US, an inhibition that no longer exists.

On the other hand, just as the Warsaw Pact has disappeared, NATO is now well advanced in the process of breaking up and going the way of SEATO and CENTO. The 1999 war against Serbia made its demise much more likely, while the US-led alliance disagreed profoundly over the Iraq War, troop commitments to Afghanistan, and the function of NATO in policing the world on the US's behalf rather than resisting a Soviet threat that no longer exists. American-led alliances such as NATO are increasingly likely to dissolve in fact, if not formally.

At least eight nations have nuclear weapons already, but the UN says another 30 or so have the skill and resources to become nuclear powers. The world is escaping from US control, but it is also escaping the forms of control that were in place when the USSR existed and states were too poor to build nuclear weapons. The world is more dangerous, in large part because the US refuses to recognize the limits of its power and retains the ambitions it had 50 years ago. But the spread of all kinds of weapons also has its own momentum – one that US arms exports aid immeasurably.

Iraq was not at the top of the Bush Administration's agenda when it came to power in 2001. It was committed, however, to a "forward-leaning" foreign policy, to use Donald Rumsfeld's words, and to greater military activism. Had the September 11 attacks not occurred, it is more likely that it would have confronted China, which has nuclear weapons but which the Administration deems a "peer competitor" in the vast East Asia region. It still may do so, although Iraq has been a total disaster – militarily and geopolitically – and alienated the US public much more quickly than the Vietnam War did. The American military is falling apart, its weapons have been ineffective, and politically Iraq is likely to break up into regional fiefdoms (as Afghanistan has) or fall into civil war – no one knows. From the Iraqi viewpoint too, the war was a disaster, but it only repeated the failures of a line of previous American presidents in Korea, Vietnam, and elsewhere.

That the Iraq resistance is divided will not save the US from defeat. Few believe Iraq will be spared great trauma. In fact, official American experts predicted this before the war began and they were ignored, just as they were ignored when they predicted disaster in Vietnam in the 1960s. We live in a tragic world where war is considered more virtuous than peace – and since arms manufacturers profit from wars and not peace, conventional wisdom is reinforced by their lobbying and preaching of the cult of weaponry. The US may explore how to end its predicament in Iraq but only Iran can help it, and geopolitically it is Iran that has gained most from Saddam Hussein's defeat. Iran has no incentive to save the Bush Administration from the losses now facing it – both in Iraq and in future elections in the US.

World opposition is decentralized to a much greater extent and the US is less than ever able to control it; indeed, in the process of seeking to maintain its hegemony it will become financially bankrupt and break up its alliances.

3
Alliances and NATO

A century before the Bush Administration made Russia an enemy by pushing NATO eastwards and proposing anti-missile systems in Poland and the Czech Republic, America believed that Russia was its potential foe. Brooks Adams and his close friend, President Theodore Roosevelt, thought there was a Slav menace and Roosevelt secretly supported the Japanese in their war with Russia in 1903. In the post-1945 period, President Truman and his advisers often relied on the will of Czar Peter the Great, a known forgery, to fathom Stalin's true intentions, placing communism in the chain of Russian expansionism. Lenin allowed the West to demonize Russia with the label of communism but after the demise of the latter the fear of Russia has remained. It has always been there.

NATO was established in April 1949 to allow the United States to impose its hegemony – political and ideological – on the West European states, and this has always been a prime factor in all of its calculations. The existence of communism in Russia was its nominal justification, but this was simply a useful excuse. Without NATO, a Western European defense alliance – a Third Force as envisaged by De Gaulle and Churchill – would have been formed independently of American membership and control. What these leaders feared most was a resurgent Germany, not the Soviet Union. Although there was concern over internal communist subversion, potential Soviet aggression was considered most unlikely – the Russians were then on a peace offensive and Washington deemed them too weak to embark on war. The US was ferociously opposed to Europe being its own master, pursuing an independent foreign policy.

Nominally, NATO was an anti-Soviet alliance, but the US planned to counter any Soviet aggression with its overwhelming nuclear superiority – for which it did not need NATO or, indeed, its own ground forces. Washington replaced Western Europe's independent conception of itself with the fear of the USSR, in response to which "Atlanticism" – protection through unity behind an American shield – became the new ideology. But once the Soviet Union ceased to exist in 1991 NATO became an anomaly. The stable world in which the behavior of the USSR was more or less predictable has been superseded by a far more dangerous world of infinite surprises, with no easily identifiable enemy to unite against.

In the late 1990s the Clinton Administration indicated that "NATO could become a relic" if the Europeans created a military organization of their own whose decisions America could not control. The issues then concerned a European Union military force not subject to a US veto and Europe's dislike of the planned – and still illusory – American missile defense system. Many European nations – Germany in particular – regard the proposed system as destabilizing and a symptom of Washington's growing unilateralism, which, it should be noted, began under the Clinton Administration. Atlanticism no longer had the same magic for a region that was becoming as powerful as the US economically, was debating the creation a common currency and stronger organizations, and for which there was no longer a communist threat to unite it behind the American shield.

Moreover, in the case of the war in Yugoslavia – the so-called Kosovo war which began in March of 1999 – all members of the NATO alliance had vetoes over American military actions, inhibiting the latter constantly. The Pentagon and the Bush Administration, long before September 11, 2001, were determined to escape NATO's cumbersome restrictions. But the maintenance of NATO as a political alliance is required to stop an independent military organization under the European Union's aegis. When the Bush Administration came to office it too was committed to doing far less in the Balkans, leaving this task to the United States' European allies.

After September 11, however, it told its European allies that while they could supply soldiers the US alone would determine how and where they would be used. Given their internal politics and their own images of themselves as world-class powers, the Germans, French, Italians, and others offered to send small numbers of armed forces to Afghanistan. But the ideology of Atlanticism still held sway over many Europeans, especially the British. At first, the Pentagon did not want to take foreign troops but did so when the war in Afghanistan became protracted. It was glad to have the extra manpower but nevertheless refused to consult NATO's members on military and political matters. The US began to worry its important NATO allies. While they have continued to provide military forces, Europe is again finding its own identity – some nations more than others.

When George Bush's Administration declared in the Quadrennial Defense Review Report of September 2001 that "America's security role in the world is unique," it saw NATO as a source of manpower, which civilian hawks such as Vice-President Dick Cheney and Donald Rumsfeld in the Defense Department regarded as indispensable for the prosecution of war in Iraq – and, possibly, in Iran, Syria, and elsewhere, once the war in Iraq was won easily. But it was to be manpower without inhibiting conditions.

Since this global vision – essentially shared by its predecessors – underscored the Bush Administration's policy, troop numbers became crucial to Washington. But now NATO's members saw Washington's demands as dangerous. The US needed manpower unconditionally, and that is why NATO is now falling apart: Germany and other key NATO members initially refused to supply the numbers required, which kept increasing as the wars in Afghanistan and Iraq dragged on and became marked by a succession of protracted failures.

There were other reasons for NATO's concern. Russia is now the world's largest supplier of gas, which has earned it the way out of its economic troubles of the 1990s. Imported gas has made European nations dependent upon Russia, just as Japan and China rely upon petroleum from Iran. Russia also has modern weapons, which it exports to anyone prepared to pay, and is extending its influence. The US not only wishes to establish anti-missile systems in Poland and Czech Republic, themselves new NATO members, but is also encouraging Georgia and the Ukraine to join the alliance. Russia regards NATO's move eastward as an extremely hostile gesture and says it will penetrate any missile shield. At the same time, NATO troops are deemed useful to the US in the war in Afghanistan, to supplement its 30,000-odd existing forces. On Iran, too, alliance members are deeply divided on the use of sanctions – the Iranians have oil and their new-found economic power makes the American-led boycott a source of dispute. Economic sanctions are failing, and European governments still provide Iran with enormous loan guarantees ($18 billion in 2005 and not much less than that now).

Numbers were still at issue in 2008, with the US failing to get the troops it thinks it needs in Afghanistan to conclude this protracted and uncertain war. Its scope now includes the tribal regions of northern Pakistan, while the Taliban is again growing in strength. Germany, especially, refused to send more soldiers, and opposes the missile defense system as well as the enlargement of NATO to include the Ukraine and Georgia, nations bordering on Russia, as provocative. The entire credibility of NATO depends on these troop commitments – but Washington will not get what it is asking for. The Bush Administration itself does not know what it needs, much less how long the war will take. Washington's diktat has ceased to rule NATO on this most critical issue. Its aspiration to political hegemony over Europe is now over. America's alliance system is ending and may indeed have ended by the time these words make it into print.

No less crucial, and perhaps decisive, is the role of Europe in the world economy. As it has become far stronger, and since the US is no longer as economically hegemonic as it was after World War II, Europe has developed an identity appropriate to its new economic power, while the emergence of China, India, Brazil, Russia, and the commodity-rich nations is now far more crucial to the international economy. American adventures in Iraq and Afghanistan are no longer relevant to Europe's priorities. They get in the way of its doing business. Likewise NATO now appears as the artifact of a Cold War era in which communism rather than business seemed more important. Europe, in brief, is attempting to find its identity, appropriate to its own interests and in the absence of communism as the unifying, obsessive bogeyman it was from 1945 until 1991. To follow America's definition of its interests, which amounts to engaging in a struggle against "terrorism" everywhere, including against nations that have oil and gas to sell, is no longer perceived as rational in Europe. We are in a period of transition.

There are also vital global dimensions of this fatal weakening of American domination, which I do not discuss in detail here. South Korea's abandonment of US control and hegemony is only one of many examples (two-way trade between South Korea and China was $145 billion in 2008). Taiwan is also a case of a Cold War hot-spot that is now being resolved because the Chinese in Taiwan want to buy Chinese stock and to do business with the "communists" and mainland businessmen, at least 20 of whom have become billionaires. China is now the third largest economy in the world and a temptation to every nation in the region – Australia included.

The following essay deals with this dissolution of US power and NATO, a crucial pillar of the American century, in the context of the presidential election of 2004.

ALLIANCES AND THE AMERICAN ELECTION
(Counterpunch, March 2004)

Alliances have been a major cause of wars throughout modern history, removing inhibitions that might otherwise have caused Germany, France, and many other nations to reflect much more cautiously before embarking on paths leading to death and destruction. The dissolution of all alliances is a crucial precondition of a world without wars.

The United States' strength, to an important extent, has rested on its ability to convince other nations that it was in their vital interests to see America prevail in its global role. With the loss of that ability there will be a fundamental change in the international system whose implications and consequences may ultimately be as far-reaching as the dissolution of the Soviet bloc. The scope of America's world mission is now far more dangerous and ambitious than when communism existed, but it was fear of the USSR that alone gave NATO its raison d'être and provided Washington with the justification for its global pretensions. Enemies have disappeared and new ones – many once former allies and congenial states – have taken their places. The United States, to a degree to which it is itself uncertain, needs alliances. But even friendly nations are less likely than ever to be bound into uncritical "coalitions of the willing."

Announced on September 19, 2002, nothing in President Bush's extraordinarily vague doctrine of fighting "preemptive" wars, unilaterally if necessary, was a fundamentally new departure. Since the 1890s, and regardless of whether Republicans or Democrats were in office, the US has intervened in countless ways in the Western Hemisphere – from sending marines to support friendly tyrants, to determining the political destinies of many nations. The Democratic Administration that established the United Nations explicitly regarded the Western Hemisphere as the US's sphere of influence, and it created the IMF and World Bank to police the world economy.

It was the Democratic Party that created most of the pillars of postwar American foreign policy, from the Truman Doctrine in 1947 and the creation of NATO through the institutionalization of the arms race and the illusion that weapons and firepower are a solution to many of the world's political problems. The Democrats share, in the name of a truly "bipartisan" consensus, equal responsibility for both the character and dilemmas of America's foreign strategy at the present moment. President Jimmy Carter initiated the Afghanistan adventure in July 1979, hoping to bog down the Soviets there as the Americans had been in Vietnam. And it was Carter who first encouraged Saddam Hussein to confront Iranian fundamentalism, a policy President Reagan continued.

Joseph E. Stiglitz, chairman of the President's Council of Economic Advisers from 1993 to 1997, argues that the Clinton Administration intensified the "hegemonic legacy" in the world economy, and that Bush is just continuing it. The 1990s was a "decade of unparalleled American influence over the global economy" that Democratic financiers and fiscal conservatives in key posts defined, "in which one economic crisis seemed to follow another." The US created trade barriers and gave large subsidies to its own agribusiness while countries in financial straits were advised, often compelled, to cut spending and "adopt policies that were markedly different from those that we ourselves had adopted."[1] The scale of domestic and global peculation by the Clinton and Bush Administrations can be debated, but it was enormous in both cases.

In foreign and military affairs, both Administrations have suffered from the same procurement fetish, believing that expensive weapons are superior to realistic political strategies. The same illusions produced the Vietnam War – and disaster. Elegant strategies promising technological routes to victory have been with us since the late 1940s, but they are essentially public relations exercises intended to encourage more orders for arms manufacturers and justifications for bigger budgets for the rival military services. During the Clinton years the Pentagon continued to concoct grandiose strategies and demanded – and got – new weapons with which to implement them. There are many ways to measure defense expenditures over time but – minor annual fluctuations notwithstanding – the consensus between the two parties on the Pentagon's budgets has persisted since 1945. In January 2000 Clinton added $115 billion to the Pentagon's 5-year plan, far more than the Republicans were calling for. When Clinton left office the Pentagon had over a half trillion dollars in the major weapons procurement pipeline, not counting the ballistic missile defense systems – which is a pure boondoggle that cost over $71 billion by 1999. The dilemma, as both CIA and senior Clinton officials correctly warned, was that terrorists were more likely to strike the American homeland than some nation against whom the military could retaliate. This fundamental disparity between hardware and reality has always existed, and September 11, 2001 showed how vulnerable and weak the US has become.[2]

The war in Yugoslavia in the spring of 1999 brought the future of NATO and the alliance, and especially Washington's deepening anxiety regarding Germany's possible independent role in Europe, to a head. Well before Bush took office, the Clinton Administration resolved never to allow its allies to inhibit or define its strategy again. Bush's policies, notwithstanding the brutal way in which they have been expressed and implemented, follow logically from this crucial decision.

But the world today is increasingly dangerous for the US, and communism's demise has called into fundamental question the core premises of the post-1945 alliance system. More nations have nuclear weapons and the means of delivering them; destructive small arms (thanks to burgeoning US arms exports which grew from 32 percent of world trade in 1987 to 43 percent in 1997) are much more abundant; there are more local and civil wars than ever, especially in regions like Eastern Europe which had not experienced any for nearly a half-century; and there is terrorism – the poor and weak man's ultimate weapon – on a scale that has never before existed. The political, economic, and cultural causes of instability and conflict are growing, and expensive weapons are irrelevant – save for the balance sheets of those who make them.

So long as the future is to a large degree – to paraphrase Defense Secretary Donald Rumsfeld – "unknowable," it is not in the national interest of the traditional US allies to perpetuate the relationships created from 1945 to 1990. The Bush Administration – through ineptness and a vague ideology of American power that acknowledges no limits on its global ambitions, and through a preference for unilateralist initiatives and adventurism which discounts consultations with its friends much less the United Nations – has seriously eroded the alliance system upon which US foreign policy from 1947 onwards was based. With the proliferation of all sorts of destructive weaponry and growing political instability the world is becoming increasingly dangerous – as is membership in alliances.

If Bush is reelected then the international order may be very different in 2008 than it is today, much less in 1999, but there is no reason to believe that objective assessments of the costs and consequences of US actions will significantly alter America's foreign policy priorities over the next four years. If the Democrats win they will attempt in the name of "progressive internationalism" to reconstruct the alliance system as it existed before the Yugoslav war of 1999, when the Clinton Administration turned against the veto powers built into the NATO system. There is important bipartisan support for resurrecting the Atlanticism that Bush is in the process of smashing, and it was best reflected in the Council on Foreign Relations' vague and banal March 2004 report on the "transatlantic alliance," which Henry Kissinger helped direct and which both influential Republicans and Wall Street leaders endorsed. Traditional elites are desperate to see NATO and the Atlantic system restored to their old glory. That same month, in a new book, Zbigniew Brzezinski, who was Carter's National Security Adviser, best articulated their vision, premised on the expansionist assumptions that have guided American foreign policy since 1945. Brzezinski is far subtler than most, and rejects the Bush Administration's counterproductive rhetoric that so alienates former and potential future allies. But he regards American power as central to peace in every part of the world and his global vision is no less ambitious than the Bush Administration's. He is for the US maintaining "a comprehensive technological edge over all potential rivals." His is a call to "transform America's prevailing power into a co-optive hegemony – one in which leadership is exercised more through shared conviction with enduring allies than by assertive domination." And because it is much more saleable to past and potential allies, this traditional Democratic vision is far more dangerous than that of the inept, eccentric mélange of men and women now guiding American foreign policy.[3]

But Vice-President Richard Cheney, Donald Rumsfeld, and the neoconservative and eclectic hawks in Bush's Administration are oblivious to the consequences of their recommendations or the way they shock America's friends overseas. Many of the President's key advisers possess aggressive, essentially academic geopolitical visions that assume overwhelming, decisive American military and economic power. Personalized interpretations of the Bible's allegedly missionary appeals inspire yet others, including Bush himself, and most utilize an amorphous nationalist and Messianic rhetoric that makes it impossible to predict exactly how Bush will mediate between very diverse, often quirky influences. Although he has so far favored advocates of the US unilaterally and wantonly employing its might throughout virtually the entire world, no one close to the President acknowledges the limits of US power – limits that are political and, as Korea and Vietnam proved, also military.

John Kerry voted for many of Bush's key foreign and domestic measures and is, at best, a very indifferent presidential candidate. His statements and interviews over the past months dealing with foreign affairs have mostly been both vague and incoherent, though he is explicitly and ardently pro-Israel and explicitly for regime-change in Venezuela. His policies on the Middle East are identical to Bush's, and this alone will prevent the alliance with Europe from being reconstructed. On Iraq, even as the violence there escalated and Kerry finally had a crucial issue over which to win the election, his position has remained indistinguishable from the President's. Until an Iraqi armed force can replace it, Kerry wrote in the *Washington Post* on April 13, the American military has to stay in Iraq – "preferably helped by NATO." "No matter who is elected president in November, we will persevere in that mission" to build a stable, pluralistic Iraq – which, I must add, has never existed and is unlikely to emerge in the foreseeable future. "It is a matter of national honor and trust." Kerry has promised to leave American troops in Iraq for his entire first term if necessary, but is vague about their subsequent departure. Not even the scandal over the treatment of Iraqi prisoners evoked Kerry's criticism, despite the fact it has profoundly alienated a politically decisive segment of the American public.

His statements on domestic policy in favor of fiscal restraint and lower deficits, much less tax breaks for large corporations, utterly lack voter appeal. Kerry is packaging himself as an economic conservative who is also strong on defense spending – a Clinton clone – because that is precisely how he feels. His advisers are the same investment bankers who helped Clinton get the nomination in 1992, raised the funds to help him get elected, and then defined his economic policy. The most important of them is Robert Rubin, who became Treasury secretary; Rubin and his cronies are running the Kerry campaign and will also dictate his economic agenda should he win. These are the same men whom Stiglitz attacks as advocates of the rich and powerful.

Kerry is, to his core, an ambitious patrician educated in elite schools and anything but a populist. He is neither articulate nor impressive as a candidate, and is unable to formulate an alternative to Bush's foreign and defense policies, which themselves still have far more in common with Clinton's than they have differences. He may be critical of Bush but this is scarcely justification for wishful thinking about Kerry, though every presidential election produces such illusions. Although the foreign and military policy goals of the Democrats and Republicans since 1947 have been essentially consensual, both in terms of objectives and the varied means – from covert to overt warfare – of attaining them, there have been significant differences in the way they were expressed. This was far less the case with Republican presidents and presidential candidates for most of the twentieth century, and men like Taft, Hoover, Eisenhower, or Nixon were very sedate by comparison to Reagan or the present rulers in Washington. But style can be important and inadvertently the Bush Administration's falsehoods, rudeness, and peremptory demands have begun to destroy an alliance system that for the sake of world peace should have been abolished long ago. In this context, it is far more likely that the nations allied with the US in the past will be compelled to stress their own interests and go their own ways. The Democrats are far less likely to continue that exceedingly desirable process, a process ultimately much more conducive to peace internationally. They will perpetuate the same adventurism and opportunism that began generations ago and that Bush has merely built upon, the same dependence on military means to solve political crises, the same interference with every corner of the globe as if America has a divinely ordained mission to interfere in all the world's problems. The Democrats' greater finesse in justifying these policies is therefore more dangerous because they will be made to seem more credible and will keep alive alliances that only reinforce the US's refusal to acknowledge the limits of its power. In the longer run, Kerry's pursuit of these aggressive goals will lead eventually to a renewal of the dissolution of alliances, but in the short run he will attempt to rebuild them – and that is to be deplored.

The Stakes for the World

Critics of American foreign policy will not rule Washington after this election regardless of who wins. As dangerous as he is, Bush's reelection is much more likely to produce the continued destruction of the alliance system that is so crucial to American power in the long run. Facts in no way imply

moral judgments if we merely identify them. One does not
have to believe that the worse is the better, but we have
to consider candidly the foreign policy consequences of a
renewal of Bush's mandate, not the least because it is likely.

Bush's policies have managed to alienate, to varying
degrees, innumerable nations, and even its firmest allies – such
as Britain, Australia, and Canada – are beginning to ask
whether giving Washington a blank check is in their national
interest or if it undermines the tenure of parties in power.
Foreign affairs, as the terrorist attack in Madrid dramatically
showed in March, are too important to uncritically endorse
American policies. Politicians who support them have been
highly vulnerable to criticism from the opposition and from
dissidents within their own ranks. And the parties in power
can pay dearly for it, as in Spain, where the people were always
overwhelmingly opposed to entering the war in Iraq and the
ruling party snatched defeat from the jaws of victory; more
important are the innumerable victims among the people.
The nations that have supported the Iraq War enthusiastically, particularly Great Britain, Italy, the Netherlands, and
Australia, have made their populations especially vulnerable
to terrorism. They now have the expensive responsibility of
protecting them – if they can.

The Washington-based Pew Research Center report on
public opinion released on March 16, 2004 showed that
a large and rapidly increasing majority of the French,
Germans, and even British want an independent European
foreign policy, a majority that reached 75 percent in France
in March 2004 compared to 60 percent two years earlier. The
US "favorability rating" plunged to 38 percent in France and
Germany. Even in Britain it fell from 75 to 58 percent and
the proportion of the population supporting the decision to

go to war in Iraq dropped from 61 percent in May 2003 to 43 percent in March 2004. Prime Minister Blair's domestic credibility, after the Labour Party was placed third in the June 10 local and European elections, is at its nadir.[4] Right after the political debacle in Spain, the president of Poland, in whose country a majority of the people has always been opposed to sending troops to Iraq or keeping them there, complained that Washington had "misled" him on Iraq's weapons of mass destruction and hinted that Poland might withdraw its 2,400 troops from Iraq earlier than previously scheduled. In Italy, by last May, 71 percent of the people favored withdrawing the 2,700 Italian troops in Iraq no later than June 30, and leaders of the main opposition have already declared they will withdraw them if they win the spring 2006 elections – a promise they and other antiwar parties in Britain and Spain used in the mid-June European Parliament elections to increase their power significantly. The issue now is whether nations like Poland, Italy, or the Netherlands can afford to isolate themselves from the major European powers and their own public opinion to remain a part of the increasingly quixotic and unilateralist American-led "coalition of the willing." The political liabilities of remaining close to Washington are obvious, the advantages non-existent.

What has happened in Spain is probably a harbinger of the future, further isolating the quixotic American government in its adventures. The Bush Administration sought to unite nations behind the Iraq War with a gargantuan lie – that Saddam Hussein had weapons of mass destruction – and failed spectacularly. Meanwhile, terrorism is stronger than ever and its proponents now have far more credibility in the Muslim world. The Iraq War energized al-Qaeda and extremism and has tied down the US, dividing its alliances as never before. Conflict in Iraq may escalate, as it has since March, creating a protracted armed conflict with Shiites and Sunnis that could last many months, even years. Will the nations that have sent troops to Iraq keep them there indefinitely, as Washington is increasingly likely to ask them to do? Can political leaders in the "coalition of the willing" afford conceding to insatiable American demands?

Elsewhere, Washington opposes the major European nations on Iran, in part because the neoconservatives and realists within its own ranks are deeply divided, and the same is true of its relations with Japan, South Korea, and China on how to deal with North Korea. America's effort to assert its moral and ideological superiority, crucial elements in its postwar hegemony, is failing – badly.

The way the war in Iraq was justified compelled France and Germany to become far more independent on foreign policy, far earlier, than they had intended or were prepared to be. The future role of NATO is now questioned in a way that was inconceivable two years ago. Europe's future defense arrangements are today unresolved, but there will be some sort of European military force independent of NATO and American control. Germany and France strongly oppose the Bush doctrine of preemption. Tony Blair, however much he intends to act as a proxy for the US on military questions, must return Britain to the European project, and his willingness since late 2003 to emphasize his nation's role in Europe reflects political necessities. To do otherwise would be to alienate his increasingly powerful neighbors and risk losing elections.

Even more dangerous, the Bush Administration has managed to turn what was in the mid 1990s a blossoming cordial friendship with the former Soviet Union into an increasingly tense relationship. Despite a 1997 non-binding American pledge not to station substantial numbers of combat troops in the territories of new members, NATO last March incorporated seven East European nations and is now on Russia's very borders. Washington is in the process of establishing an undetermined but significant number of bases in the Caucasus and Central Asia. Russia has stated repeatedly that the US encroachment requires that it remain a military superpower and modernize its delivery systems so as to be more than a match for the increasingly expensive and ambitious missile defense system and space weapons the Pentagon is now building. Russia has 5,286 nuclear warheads and 2,922 intercontinental missiles. There is a dangerous and costly renewal of the arms race now occurring.

In February of this year Russia threatened to pull out of the crucial Conventional Forces in Europe Treaty, which has yet to enter into force, because it regards America's ambitions in the former Soviet bloc as provocation. "I would like to remind the representatives of [NATO]," Defense Minister Sergei Ivanov told a security conference in Munich last February, "that with its expansion they are beginning to operate in the zone of vitally important interests of our country." And by increasingly acting unilaterally without United Nations authority – where Russia's seat on the Security Council gives it a veto power that, in Ivanov's words, is one of the "major factors for ensuring global stability" – the US has made international relations "very dangerous."[5] The question Washington's allies will ask themselves is whether their traditional alliances now entail far more risks than benefits – and if they are still necessary.

In the case of China, Bush's key advisers publicly assigned the highest priority to confronting its burgeoning military

and geopolitical power the moment they came to office.
But China's military budget is growing rapidly – 12 percent
this coming year – and the European Union wants to lift its
15-year-old arms embargo and get a share of the enticingly
large market. The Bush Administration, of course, is strongly
resisting any relaxation of the export ban. Establishing bases
on China's western borders is the logic of its ambitions.

By installing bases in small or weak Eastern European
and Central Asian nations, the US is not so much engaged
in "power projection" against an amorphously defined
terrorism as once more confronting Russia and China in an
open-ended context which may have profoundly serious and
protracted consequences that neither America's allies nor its
own people will have any inclination to support. Even some
Pentagon analysts have warned against this strategy because
any American attempt to save failed states in the Caucasus
or Central Asia, implicit in its new obligations, will risk
exhausting what are ultimately its finite military resources.[6]
The political crisis now wracking Uzbekistan makes this fear
very real.

There is no way to predict what emergencies will arise or
what these commitments will entail, either for the US or its
allies, not least because – as Iraq proved last year and Vietnam
long before it – America's intelligence on the capabilities and
intentions of potential enemies against which it is ready to
strike preemptively is so completely faulty. Without accurate
information a state can believe and do anything, and this
is the predicament the Bush Administration's allies are in.
It is simply not in their national interest, much less in the
political interests of those now in power or the security of
their people, to pursue foreign policies based on a blind,
uncritical acceptance of fictions or a flamboyant adventurism
premised on false premises and information. It is far too open-

ended both in terms of the potential time and political costs involved. If Bush is reelected, America's allies and friends will have to confront such stark choices; a painful process that will redefine and probably shatter existing alliances. Many nations, including the larger, powerful ones, will embark on independent, realistic foreign policies, and the dramatic events in Spain have reinforced this likelihood.

The United States will be more prudent, and the world will be far safer, only if it is constrained by a lack of allies and isolated. And that is happening.

4
Israel:
A Stalemated Accident of History

In late 1949 I worked on a boat taking Jews from Marseilles to Haifa, Israel. Jews from Arab nations were in the front of the boat, Europeans in the rear. I was regarded by many of the Europeans as some sort of freak because I had a United States passport and so could stay in the land of milk and honey. One man wanted me to marry his daughter – which meant he too could live in that land of plenty. My Hebrew became quite respectable but the experience was radicalizing or, I should say, kept me radical, and I have stayed that way.

Later I learned from someone who ran a displaced persons camp in Germany that the large majority of Jews wanted to go anywhere but Palestine. They were compelled to choose Palestine or else risk receiving no aid. I understood very early that there was much amiss in the countless Arab villages and homes I saw destroyed, and that the entire Zionist project – regardless of the often venal nature of the Arab opposition to it – was a dangerous sham.

The result of the creation of a state called Israel was abysmal. Jews from Poland have nothing in common with Jews from Germany and neither has anything to do with those from the Arab world. It is nationality, not religion, that counts most. Jews in Israel, especially the Germans, largely ghettoized themselves by their place of origin during the first generation, when a militarized culture produced the mixed new breed called *sabras* – an essentially anti-intellectual personality far different from the one the early Zionists, who were mostly socialists who preached the nobility of labor, expected to emerge. The large majority of Israelis are not in the least Jewish in the cultural sense, are scarcely socialist in any sense, and daily life and the way people live is no different in Israel than it is in Chicago or Amsterdam. There is simply no rational reason that justifies the state's creation. The outcome is a small state with a military ethos that pervades all aspects of Israel's culture, its politics and, above all, its response to the existence of Arabs in its midst and at its borders. From its inception, the ideology of the early Zionists – of Labor Zionism as well as the rightist Revisionism that Vladimir Jabotinsky produced – embodied a commitment to violence, erroneously called self-defense, and a virtual hysteria. As a transcendent idea, Zionism has no validity because the national differences between Jews are overwhelming.

What Zionism confirmed, if any confirmation were needed, is that accidents are more important in shaping history than is all too often allowed. Here was the intellectual café, which existed in key cities – Vienna at the turn of the twentieth century or the Lower East Side of New York before World War I – filled with immensely creative people full of ideas and longing for a golden era to come. Ideas – good, bad, and indifferent – flourished. In this heady atmosphere, Zionism was born.

But Zionism has produced a Sparta that traumatized an already artificially divided region, partitioned after the collapse of the Ottoman Empire during World War I led to the Versailles Treaty and the creation of the modern Middle East. The state of Israel has always relied on military solutions to political and sociological problems with the Arabs. The result is constant mobilization.

Even more troublesome for peace and stability in the vast Middle East, Zionism has always been symbiotic with some great power for the security of its national project, realized in a state called Israel. Before 1939 it was the British; during the 1950s it was France. Israel has survived since the late 1960s on the influx of US arms and money, and this has allowed it to encourage its fears of annihilation – a fate its possession of nuclear weapons makes most unlikely. But Israel also has an importance far beyond the fantasies of a few confused literati. Today its significance for American foreign policy is far greater because the Soviet Union no longer exists and the Middle East provokes the fear so essential to mobilizing Congress and the US public. "The best hopes and the worst fears of the planet are invested in that relatively small patch of earth" – as George Tenet, the former head of the CIA, put it in his memoir – and so understanding how and why that patch came into being, and the grave limits of the martial course it is following, has a very great, even transcendent value.[1]

In July 2003 Foreign Minister Shalom predicted that Iran would have nuclear bomb capability by 2006. It did not have nuclear weapons in 2006, though in fact a successful strike by conventional missiles on Dimona, Israel's nuclear facility, would radioactivate a good part of Israel – and both Iran and Syria have such missiles. Defense Minister Ehud Barak, during Vice-President Dick Cheney's visit in late March 2008, stated that "Iran's weapons programme threatens not only the stability of the region, but of the whole world," and he did not rule out a war with it. By spring 2008 Israel was also very concerned about the growing ascendancy of Hizbollah in Lebanon and its greatly increased firepower – mainly in the form of rockets capable of striking much of Israel. It regards Hizbollah as a tool of Iran, and its focus on Iran concerns its control over Hizbollah as well as its ability to challenge Israel's nuclear monopoly. But there can be no doubt that Hizbollah's strength has only grown since Israel attacked it in Lebanon in the summer of 2006. Israel now has an enemy that can inflict immense damage on it, probably resulting in highly skilled Jews migrating far faster than they already are at present – even now, more Jews are leaving Israel than migrating to it.

The existence of Israel is scarcely the only reason American policy in the region is as bad as it is. After all, it did not take Zionism to encourage Washington to seek the elimination of British influence in the region, and today no one can tell how long the US will remain mired in the affairs of the Middle East. But Israel is now a vital factor. While the extent of its role can be debated, without Israel the politics of the entire Middle East would be different – troubled but very different.

At least equally nefarious in the long run, Israel's existence has radicalized – but in a negative sense – the Arab world, distracting it from natural class differences that often overcome religious and tribal ties. It has fanned Arab nationalism abysmally and given it a transcendent negative identity.

I am very realistic – and pessimistic – about an eventual negotiated solution to the crisis that has surrounded Palestine and Israel. Given the magnitude of the changes needed, the present situation justifies the most dismal conclusions. After all, the Arabs that live under Israeli control will quite soon outnumber the Jewish population, leaving a de facto Jewish state in which Jews are a minority! This fact is becoming deeply troublesome within Israeli politics today, causing former expansionists to reverse their position and leading to more and more internal controversy. Nor will there ever be an administration in Washington ready to do diplomatically what none has ever dared do since 1947, namely compel Israel to make an equitable peace with the Arabs.

Neither a one- nor two-state solution will come to pass. But the Jewish population is very likely to decline, and if it falls sufficiently then demography may prove to be a crucial factor. The ratio of Jews to Arabs would then become highly significant. The Jews in Israel are highly skilled and many have gotten out, migrating abroad. The Israeli military is the most powerful in the region because it has been deluged with American equipment, which it has learned to service. But US forces need repairmen to service the very same equipment, more than ever because recruitment into the American military is now lower than it has been in a quarter-century (not to mention the military's high suicide rate), and skilled Israelis can take jobs with America's armed forces that they are eminently qualified to fill. Moreover, Iran and the other Arab states will eventually develop or acquire nuclear weapons, making Israel incredibly insecure for its highly mobile Jewish population – one exhausted by regular service in compulsory reserves. And as already suggested, destroying Dimona with conventional missiles or mortars would be a cheap way to radioactivate a good part of Israel. Even worse, Osama bin Laden, or someone like him, may acquire a nuclear device, and one nuclear bomb detonated in or near Israel will effectively destroy what is a tiny area. Whoever destroys Israel will be proclaimed a hero in the Arab world. To those with skills, the answer is clear: get out. And getting out they are.

There are also Orthodox Jews in Israel but Israeli mass culture is now virtually indistinguishable from consumerism anywhere – in many crucial respects, there is more Judaism in parts of Brooklyn or Toronto than in most of Israel. The Orthodox too may be ready to leave behind the insecurity and troubles confronting those who live in a nation that is, after all, a part of a highly unstable region.

Sober and quite rational Israelis exist, of course, and I cite them often enough, but American policy will be determined by factors having nothing to do with them. Unfortunately, rational Israelis are an all too small minority. The articles that follow deal with the most crucial dimensions of Israel's failures and their causes. There is some overlap here with my essay on Iran and Israel in the following chapter. Together, they get at some of the roots of the problem called Israel. I should make it quite clear, however, that these essays hardly exhaust the complexity of American foreign policy with respect to the migration of Jews to Palestine or its present support for Israel, which began in earnest only in the late 1960s. Under President Franklin D. Roosevelt, from 1933 to 1945, very few German Jews attempting to escape Nazi persecution, which led inevitably to the Holocaust, were allowed to enter the US. Only those with special skills or family connections could do so. Oil, particularly in Saudi Arabia, defined American policy in the Middle East, and the Roosevelt Administration opposed Zionist claims to Palestine. I have detailed this earlier US position in my book *The Politics of War*, published in 1968. Much more than the 1924 American immigration law was involved in ensuring that the flow of Jews to Palestine became so substantial, but it was nonetheless very important and deserves much more attention. But I shall not burden readers here with the complexities of modern history.

ISRAEL:
MYTHOLOGIZING A TWENTIETH-CENTURY ACCIDENT
(ZNet, June 2007)

One of the many quirks of the nineteenth century's intellectual heritage was the great intensification of nationalism and, to cite Benedict Anderson, the creation of "nation-ness,"[2] the consequences of which have varied dramatically from the negligible to the crucial, at times affecting, as in the case of Israel, war and peace in a vast strategic region. There was, of course, often a basis for various nationalisms to build upon, but the essentially artificial function of forming nations out of very little or nothing was common throughout the globe. This process initially occurred mainly among intellectuals, who constructed nations in their own mind. Minorities, such as the Sunnis in Iraq, used nationalism to occlude their own inferior numerical status and run the country, while in countless other places the masses retained loyalties only to their own linguistic group, tribe, and the like. There was therefore an important class difference in the origins of these ideas. The negative reaction against foreign intrusions, whether they occurred in the Middle East, South Asia or China, ultimately failed to wipe out these local ties permanently. Such bonds often resurrected themselves.

Wars were the most conducive to this enterprise, and the emergence of what was termed socialism after 1914, which had a crucial nationalist basis in such places as China and Vietnam, was due to the fact that foreign invasions greatly magnified nationalism's ability to build on ephemeral foundations to merge socialism and patriotism. For a vital component of nationalism, often its sole one, was a hatred of foreigners, giving it largely a negative function rather than an assertion of distinctive values and traits essential to a unique entity. Myths, often far-fetched and irrational, were created. Zionism is the focus of this discussion, but it was scarcely the only example. In fact, it is merely one phase of the modern historical experience, though it has been one of the most troublesome.

Vienna was surely the most intellectually creative place in the world at the end of the nineteenth century. Economics, art, philosophy, political theories on the Right as well as Left, psychoanalysis – Vienna gave birth to or influenced most of them. Ideas had to be highly original to be noticed, and most were. We must understand the unique and rare innovative environment in which Theodore Herzl, an assimilated Hungarian Jew who became the founder of Zionism, functioned. He was, for a time, also a German nationalist with an admiration for Richard Wagner and Martin Luther. Herzl was many things, including a very efficient organizer, but he was also deeply conservative and feared that, without a state, Jews – especially those in Russia – would become revolutionaries.

A state based on religion rather than the will of all of its inhabitants was, at the end of the nineteenth century, not only a medieval notion but also a very eccentric idea, one Herzl concocted in the rarified environment of cafés where ideas were produced with scant regard for reality. It was also full of countless contradictions, rooted not merely in the conflicts between theological dogmas and democracy but also in the vast cultural differences among Jews, all of which were to appear later. Europe's Jews have precious little in common, and their mores and languages are very distinct. But the gap between Jews from Europe and those from the Arab world was far, far greater. Moreover, there were many radically different kinds of Zionists within the small movement, ranging from the religiously motivated to Marxists influenced by Tolstoy and ecology who wanted to cease being Jews altogether and, as Ber Borochov would have it, become "normal." In the end, all that was to unite Israel was a military ethic premised on a hatred of others around them; Israel was to become a warrior-state, a virtual Sparta dominated by its army. Initially, at least, Herzl had the fate of Russian and East European Jews in mind; the outcome was very different.

Zionism was an original movement, but at the turn of the century its following was close to non-existent (an important exception being the interest shown by Lord Rothschild). Moreover, from its inception Zionism was symbiotic with the Great Powers, principally Great Britain, who saw it as a way of spreading their colonial ambitions to the Middle East. As early as 1902 Herzl met with Joseph Chamberlain, then British Colonial Secretary, to further Zionist claims in the region bordering Egypt, and the following year he hired David Lloyd George, later to become prime minister, to handle the Zionist case.[3] Herzl also unsuccessfully asked the sultan of the Ottoman Empire if he might obtain Palestine, after which he advocated establishing a state in Uganda, although his followers much preferred the Holy Land. It was the principle of a Jewish state, located anywhere, that appealed to him, and mainly for Jews in the Russian Empire. Herzl was only the first in the Zionist tradition of advocating a state for other Jews; he was never in favor of all Jews moving there. Chaim Weizmann wrote Herzl in 1903 that the large majority of the young Jews in Russia were anti-Zionist because they were revolutionaries – which only reinforced Herzl's convictions. In 1913 British Intelligence estimated that perhaps 1 percent of the Jews had Zionist affiliations, a figure that rose in the Russian Pale – which contained about 6 million Jews – as the war became longer.

It was scarcely an accident that in November 1917 Lord Arthur Balfour, in a letter to Rothschild, was to express Britain's historic endorsement of a Jewish homeland in their newly mandated territory of Palestine. Some of these Englishmen also shared the Biblical view that it was the destiny of Jews to return to their ancient soil. Others thought that this gesture would help keep Russia in the war, and that there were nefarious Jews who had the influence to do so. Most saw a Jewish state as a means of consolidating British power in the vast Islamic region.[4]

Jewish Migration: Many Promised Lands

Migration has been a universal phenomenon of world history since time immemorial, and we know a great deal about its causes and motives. People migrate mainly out of necessity, generally economic, and they choose from the existing options. They very rarely go someplace for the blessings of liberty, or for ideological reasons; if they did, such variable factors as economic deprivation or changes in laws would not be relevant. In the case of Palestine and Zionism, Jews behaved like people everywhere and at most times.

It is a Zionist myth that there were many Jews who wished to emigrate to a primitive, hot, and dusty place and hence did so. They did not, and all of the available data prove this conclusively. After the Bolshevik Revolution of October 1917 the Pale was abolished and a very large number of the Jews moved to Russia's cities; many of them saw the Bolsheviks as liberators and they filled the ranks of the revolution at every level.[5] If they emigrated, and here the numbers are very important, it was not – if they had a choice – to Palestine.

From 1890 to 1924 about 2 million of the 20 million immigrants to the US were Jews, overwhelmingly from East Europe. Other nations in the Western Hemisphere also attracted about a million Jews during this period, to which we must add Jewish migration to South Africa, Australia, and the like. This does not mean that these Jews were not Zionists, only that they had no intention of embarking on *aliyah* – of going to Palestine themselves. As Herzl had believed, this was a project for others.

Jews in the Diaspora, like most ethnic groups, banded together in numerous organizations, and nostalgia and confusion soon overwhelmed them. Organized Zionism grew stronger in the US as it had not in Eastern Europe – but it demanded only money, thereby ultimately making the state of Israel viable, and eventually giving the American Jewish community immense political importance in determining who received the Democratic Party nomination for president.

In 1893 there were an estimated 10,000 Jews in Palestine, 61,000 by 1920, and 122,000 in 1925. All of these figures are only the best-informed estimates; there were censuses in 1922 and 1931 only, and even the 1922 numbers are contested. But the general trend is beyond doubt and very clear. For every Jew who went to Palestine from 1890 to 1924, at least 27 went to the Western Hemisphere. The Zionist project was the utopian dream of a tiny minority and it would have failed entirely save for two factors. The first, of course, was the Holocaust, but at least as important was the much-overlooked fact that in 1924 the US passed a new immigration law based on quotas using the nationalities distribution in the 1890 census as a basis, effectively cutting off migration from Eastern and Southern Europe to a mere trickle compared to what it had been.

In 1924, the Jewish population in Palestine increased by 5.9 percent but in 1925 – the first year the American law came into effect – it leaped 28 percent, and another 23 percent in 1926. This was still a small minority of the Jews who left Europe, but this sudden spurt was directly related to American policy. From 1927 to 1932 it never grew more than 5.3 percent annually and in 1927 it was a mere 0.2 percent.[6] Very few Jews went to Palestine, and only a small proportion of them were ideologically motivated; the vast majority of Jews migrated elsewhere.

The British had always been in favor of Jewish migration, which increased greatly after 1933. Jews formed 6 percent of the Palestinian population in 1912 but 29 percent by 1935 – but now increasingly composed of Jews from Germany rather than Poland. These Jews had to get out of Germany, where the Zionist movement had always been very weak, and they were scarcely ideological zealots. Had there been open migration to the US they would have gone there. Arab riots after 1935 compelled the British to reduce the inflow and in 1939 they adopted a White Paper enforcing strict restrictions on immigration.

What is certain is that Hitler's importance must always be set in a larger context. Without him there would never have been a flow of Jews out of Germany, and very probably no state of Israel, but the US 1924 Immigration Act was no less vital, and it would be an abstract, futile exercise to try to rank the causal factors in importance. US immigration restrictions came first, and in the vast majority of cases migrants went to Palestine out of necessity, not choice. Both of these factors were crucial: without either of them, the Zionist project of creating a Jewish state in Palestine would have remained another exotic Viennese concoction, never to be realized, because while the Jews in the Diaspora were in favor of a Jewish state, virtually none living in safe nations were ever to uproot themselves and embark on *aliyah* – the return to the ancient homeland. They had no reason to do so.

There were many promised lands and Herzl's exotic ruminations were hardly the main inspiration for the flow of Jews out of Europe. Israel's existence was an unpredictable accident of history. The past century has been full of such accidents, everywhere.

That is why the world is in such a perilous condition.

ISRAEL'S LAST CHANCE
(Antiwar.com, March 17, 2007)

The United States has given Israel $51.3 billion in military grants since 1949, most of it since 1974 – more than to any other country in the post-1945 era. Israel has also received $11.2 billion in loans for military equipment, plus $31 billion in economic grants, not to mention loan guarantees or joint military projects. Israel has, in addition, acquired the most modern American nuclear and aviation technology, and missile defense systems. It is on a par with the US in virtually every regard. In August 2007, military aid to Israel was increased by 25 percent and will total $30 billion over the next decade. But major conditions on these military grants have meant that 74 percent of the funds have remained in the US, being used to purchase American arms. Since this creates jobs and profits in many districts, Congress is more than ready to respond to the cajoling of the Israel lobby. This vast sum has both enabled and forced Israel to prepare to fight an American-style war. And yet the US since 1950 has failed to win any of its big wars, and the Iraq and Afghan wars will be the most expensive in American history.

In early 2005 the new chief of staff of the Israel Defense Forces, Dan Halutz, embarked on the most extensive reorganization in the history of the IDF. Halutz is an air force general enamored with the kind of doctrines that justify the ultra-modern equipment the Americans shower upon the Israelis. Attack helicopters, unmanned aircraft, advanced long-range intelligence and communications and the like were at the top of his agenda. His was merely a variation of Donald Rumsfeld's "shock and awe" concept.

The 34-day war in Lebanon, starting July 12, 2006, was a disastrous turning point for Israel. Until the Eliyahu Winograd Commission, which Olmert set up in September 2006, delivers its interim report in April – which will cover the first five days of the war only – and resolves these matters, we will not know precisely the orders sent to specific units or the timing of all of the actions, but there is already a consensus on far more important fundamentals. But the Israelis did not lose the war because of orders given or not given to various officers. It was a war of choice, and was planned as an air war with very limited ground incursions in the expectation that Israeli casualties would be very low. Major General Herzl Sapir, at the end of February 2007, said that "the war began at our initiative and we did not take advantage of the benefits granted to the initiator." Planning for the war began in November 2005 but had reached a high gear by the following March before the kidnapping of two IDF soldiers – the nominal excuse for the war. There is no controversy over the fact that it was a digitized, networked war, the first in Israel's experience, and conformed to Halutz' and American theories of how war is fought in this high-tech era. The US is fighting identical wars in Afghanistan and Iraq – and is in the process of losing both.

What were the Israeli objectives – war aims, if you will? While the Winograd Commission report may clarify this question, a number of goals are known already. Halutz wanted to "shock and awe" the Hizbollah and their allies with Israeli power – all within a few days. There were lesser aims, such as moving the Hizbollah rockets well away from the borders, or even getting its two kidnapped soldiers returned, but at the very least Halutz wanted to make a critical point.

Instead, he revealed Israel's vulnerability due, in large part, to the fact that the enemy was far better prepared and motivated, and more appropriately equipped. It was the end of a crucial myth, the harbinger of yet more bloody, and equal, armed conflicts or of a balance of power conducive to negotiations.[7] There are many reasons why the Israelis lost the war in Lebanon, but there is general agreement within Israel that the war ended in disaster and the deterrent value of the once unbeatable IDF has been gravely diminished in the entire Arab world for the first time since 1947. But the Israelis were defeated for many of the same reasons the Americans are losing the wars in Iraq and Afghanistan – and lost in Vietnam as well. Both their doctrine and equipment were ill-suited for the realities they confronted. There was no centralized command structure to destroy, only small groups that were lightly armed, mobile, and decentralized, able to harass and ultimately to prevail. The Hizbollah also had highly effective Russian anti-tank missiles, and the IDF admits that "several dozen" tanks were put out of commission, if not destroyed, including the Merkava Mark IV, which Israel claims is the best-protected tank in the world and which it seeks to export. Hizbollah also fired around 4,000 rockets at Israeli population centers and the IDF could not stop this demoralizing harassment. Hizbollah bunkers and arsenals were largely immune to air attacks, which caused the Israelis to "stretch the target envelope" to attack densely populated areas, causing over 1,000 civilian deaths. "Israel lost the war in the first three days," an American military expert concluded, expressing a consensus shared by many US air force analysts. "If you have that kind of surprise and you have that kind of firepower you had better win. Otherwise, you're in for the long haul."

The problem was not merely a new Arab prowess, though their improvements in morale and military organization should not be minimized. Halutz' drastic reorganization of the IDF since early 2005, which was supposed to realize the promise of all its American-supplied equipment, "caused," in General Sapir's words, "a terrible distortion." The IDF was an organizational mess, demoralized as never before, and on January 17, 2007 Halutz resigned, the first head of the IDF to voluntarily step down because of his leadership in war. Had he not resigned he would have been fired. His successor quickly annulled his reorganization of the IDF, which is now sorely disorganized. The American way of warfare had failed.

The Next War

The Lebanon war is only a harbinger of Israeli defeats to come. For the first time there is a rough equivalence in military power. Technology everywhere is now moving far faster than diplomatic and political resources or the will to control its inevitable consequences. Hizbollah has more and far better rockets than it had a few years ago – over 10,000 short-range rockets is one figure given – and Israel's military intelligence believes Hizbollah has more firepower than it had last spring, before it was attacked. Israel has failed to convince Russia not to sell or give their highly effective anti-tank missiles to nations or movements in the region. They fear that even Hamas will acquire them. Syria is procuring "thousands" of advanced anti-tank missiles from Russia, which can be fired from five kilometers away, as well as far more effective rockets that can hit Israeli cities.

If the problem of confronting the mounting dangers and limits of military technology is not resolved soon there is nothing more than wars to look forward to. The IDF intelligence branch does not think a war with Syria is likely in 2007; other Israeli military commentators think that any war with Syria would produce, at best, a bloody standoff – just like the war in Lebanon last summer. Israel has about 3,700 tanks and they are all now highly vulnerable. Its ultra-modern air arm, most of which the US has provided, only kills people but it cannot attain victory.

The New Israel: A 'Normal' Nation

In the past, wars produced victories and more territory for the Jews; now they will only produce disasters for everybody. The Lebanon war proved that.

Zionism was a concoction of Viennese coffee houses, Tolstoy's idealization of labor, early ecological sentiment in the form of the *wandervogel* that influenced Zionism, but also of various fascistic movements, militarism, and varieties of socialism including Bolshevism. Jews sought to go to Palestine not only because of the Holocaust but also due to the changes in American immigration laws in the first half of the 1920s. Without the vast sums the Diaspora provided, Zionism would never have come to fruition. Every nation has its distinctive personality reflecting its traditions and pretensions. History is capricious, and in this regard Israel is no different. It exists but it is becoming increasingly dangerous to world peace – and to itself.

Zionism always had a military ethos, imposed only in part by Arab hostility, and from the inception of Zionism's history its political and military leaders were one and the same. Generals were heroes and they did well in politics. The logic of force merged with an essentially Western, colonialist bias. Israel's founders were Europeans, and it was an outpost of European culture until the globalization of values and products made these cultural distinctions increasingly irrelevant. It always has been a militarist society, proud of its fighters. And notwithstanding the Cold War and the increasing flow of arms from the US, which, merged with its élan, meant it won all its post-1947 wars until last summer, it still retains a strong element of hysteria about the world it faces. And it is often messianic – especially its politicians – because messianism is highly influential among a growing portion of the religious and traditional population.

Israel has ceased being "Zionist" in the original sense of that ideology. For the sake of ceremony it retains Zionism as a label, just as many actual or aspiring nations have maintained various myths which justify their claims to a national identity. But it has moved a long way from the original Zionist premises, in large part because its wars with its neighbors, especially the Arabs who live in its midst or nearby, have made its military ethos dominant over everything else.

Israel today is well on its way to becoming a failed state. Were it not for the fact that this outpost of fewer than 5 million Jews is a critical factor affecting war and peace in a much larger and vital region it would not be important or at all unusual. But it is terribly confused and has a very mixed identity. The US has since the late 1960s protected it. World peace now depends on this place, its idiosyncrasies, personality, and growing contradictions.

Israel is a profoundly divided society and its politicians are venal cynics. Many nations – including surely the Palestinian leaders until Hamas, by default, took over – are no different. As Shlomo Ben-Ami, the former foreign minister, describes it, on the one side there are the economically disadvantaged Oriental Jews, Russian nationalists who were motivated above all by a desire to leave the USSR (an appreciable minority of whom are not actually Jewish), and Orthodox Jews of every sort united only by their intense dislike of "assimilationists"; on the other side we have secular Jews, some Leftists and modernizers, more skilled and of East European parentage, who were once crucial in the formation of Zionism. There are an increasing number of "Jerusalem-Jews," as Ben-Ami calls them, motivated primarily by economic incentives, and they are bringing the Right to power more and more often. They fear the Arabs who live in Israel. "Tel Aviv" Jews are assimilating to a global, modernizing culture, more akin to the "normal" existence the early Zionists preached, and they are also the most likely to emigrate because they have high skills. Israel now has as many people migrating from it as to it, and North America alone is home to up to a million of them.

Indications of these trends range from the banal to the tragic. There are all varieties of punks, gays, and so on. As for the ultra-Orthodox, some have placed "curses" on those who advocate disengaging from any settlements in the West Bank or Gaza; they will be punished by heaven. One of four ultra-Orthodox Jews believes this is precisely why Sharon was struck with a coma. Martin van Creveld, professor of military history at the Hebrew University and friend of many IDF leaders, whose fame was made studying the role of morale in armies, thinks the morale of the conscripts in the IDF is "almost to the vanishing point; in some cases crybabies have taken the place of soldiers." "Feminism" in the armed forces has intensified the rot, but "social developments" have destroyed much of the army – as have officers "who stayed behind their computers" last summer.

Never before has Israel been wracked by so many demoralizing scandals. The president of Israel resigned because of rape charges against him; Prime Minister Olmert is being investigated by the comptroller's office on four charges of corruption; the new chief of police was once accused of accepting bribes and fraud and his appointment has created an uproar; and there are plenty of other sordid cases too numerous to cite. Israel is "stewing in its own rot," a *Ha'aretz* writer concluded. The police – retired judge Vardi Zeiler commented after heading a committee to investigate the state's operation – were like Sicily and the state was on its way to becoming a mafia-style regime.

In this anarchy, wars are motivated for political reasons but are lost because the society is disintegrating and – again to quote a *Ha'aretz* writer – the government "lacks both direction and a conscience." In terms of political intelligence, Olmert can really only be compared to Bush. There is a consensus among Israeli strategists that the Iraq War was a disaster for Israel, a geopolitical gift to Iran that will leave Israel in ever-greater danger long after the Americans go home. "Israel has nothing to gain from a continued American presence in Iraq," the director of the Institute for National Security

Studies of Tel Aviv University stated last January. The US ousted the Taliban from Afghanistan and Saddam Hussein from Iraq and thereby created an overwhelming Iranian strategic domination. The US campaign for democracy has brought Hamas to power in Palestine. "It's a total misreading of reality," one Israeli expert is quoted as saying, discussing America's role in the region. American policies have failed and Israel has given carte blanche to a strategy that leaves it more isolated than ever.

Notwithstanding this consensus, on March 12 Olmert told the American–Israel Public Affairs annual conference by video link that "Those who are concerned for Israeli security should recognize the need for American success in Iraq and responsible exit." "Any outcome that will not help America's strength would undercut America's ability to deal effectively with the threat posed by the Iranian regime." His foreign minister was even stronger. "Stay the hell out of it," a *Ha'aretz* writer concluded. Few groups are more antiwar than American Jews; Congress – in its own inept way – is trying to bring the war to an end; his own strategists think the Iraq War was a disaster, and Olmert endorses Bush's folly.

The Syrian Option

It is in this context that the peace of the region will or will not evolve. Olmert will do what is best for his political position domestically, and retaining power will be his priority – no less than his predecessors and most politicians everywhere. It is not at all promising. But for technical, social, and morale reasons, Israel will not win another war. At every level, it has become far weaker. It can inflict frightful damage on its enemies but it cannot change the fundamental balance of forces that lead to victory.

Making peace with Syria would be a crucial first step for Israel, and although the Palestinian problem would remain it would nonetheless vastly improve Israeli security and disprove the Bush Administration's contention until very recently that negotiations with Syria or Iran on any Middle East question involves conceding to evil. The Israeli press reported in great detail the secret 2004–5 Israel–Syria negotiations, which were very advanced and involved major Syrian concessions – especially on water and Syrian neutrality in a host of political controversies with the Palestinians and Iranians. It also reported that Washington followed these talks closely and that Cheney's office especially opposed bringing them to a successful conclusion. At the end of January 2007 many important members of the Israeli foreign policy establishment publicly urged reopening these talks.

Olmert dismissed Syria's gestures categorically after they became public. "Don't even think about it," was Secretary of State Rice's view of a treaty when she saw Israeli officials in mid February. But though Mossad supports the obdurate Rice–Olmert view, military intelligence argues that Syria's offers are sincere and serious. Moreover, the head of military intelligence warned that Syria is growing stronger, and advised that peace was very much in the Israeli interest. He was supported by most of the foreign and defense ministries, including Minister of Defense Amir Peretz. Olmert demanded, and got, their acquiescence.[8]

A treaty could be finalized with Syria within four to six months, claimed Alon Liel, former director general of the Israeli Foreign Ministry who negotiated with the Syrians, as reported in the *Washington Times* on March 7. Liel was asked to come to the US embassy in Tel Aviv about this time and tell the entire political staff about his talks. The reports in *Ha'aretz*, which included the draft treaty, were by then quite definitive. Then the Knesset, Israel's parliament, invited Ibrahim Suleiman, Syria's representative to the talks, to speak to the foreign affairs and defense committees. Such invitations are very rare, not least because Syria and Israel are legally in a state of war. But if the Syrians and Israelis go to war again, the normally hawkish Martin van Creveld concluded at this time, Israel "could wreak much destruction, but it could not force a decision." In three or four years the Syrians would be ready for a protracted war that would prove too much for Israel. After running through his bizarre alternatives, and the state of the IDF's morale, van Creveld concluded that reaching a peace with Syria was very much to Israeli interests – and that even the Americans were coming round to the position that talking to Syria and Iran (as the Baker–Hamilton panel had recommended last December) was rational.

Syria has been desperately attempting to improve its relations with Washington, if only to forestall some mad act on the part of the US. When Israel attacked Lebanon in July 2006, Elliott Abrams, in charge of the Middle East at the National Security Council, along with other neocons in Washington, urged it to expand the war to Syria. At the end of February Syria renewed its appeal to the US to discuss any and all Middle East issues with it in "a serious and profound dialogue." For over two years it has made similar attempts; Baker knew all about these. Talking to alleged adversaries is perhaps the most fundamental point of difference between Cheney, and his neocon alliance, and Rice, and it covers North Korea, Iran, and many other places. The debate is less about the nature and goals of American foreign policy than how to conduct it – by the application of material power and the threat of war or by more traditional means, such as diplomacy. In the past several weeks, taking her cue from the Republican Establishment in the Iraq Study Group last December, Rice has been winning points in this debate, but her successes are fragile. Cheney is a powerful, determined, and cunning man who knows how to prevail all too well with the President.

America's overwhelming problems are Iraq and, above all, Iran, and apparently the Bush Administration has now decided that Syria can help it in the region. Ellen Sauerbrey, an Assistant Secretary of State, was in Damascus on March 12 nominally to discuss refugees, but she heard from the Syrians "that all the questions are linked in the Arab region and that a comprehensive dialogue is needed on all these questions." Syria has also mobilized the European Union, which now favors a return of the Golan Heights to it. On March 13 the US ambassador to Israel publicly and falsely stated that the Americans had never "expressed an opinion on what Israel should or should not do with regard to Syria."

It is now entirely in the hands of the Olmert government whether to negotiate with Syria, although the vast majority of the Israeli public is against a full withdrawal from the Golan.

Israel has ignored Washington on several very important issues, starting with the Sinai campaign in 1956, and acted in its own self-interest. The Americans were Olmert's alibi but he can use them no more. There are other crucial issues, such as the Saudi plan for the resolution of the Palestine question, and never has Israel had a greater need for peace than at the present. Instead, as in the US, its head of state may be the worst in its history, motivated by short-term political advantage and a consummate desire to retain power.

But the Syrian option is there for the taking. If there is war then the brain-drain out of Israel will accelerate and migration inwards will fall; demography will take over. Israel will then become the only place in the world where a Jew is in danger precisely because he or she is a Jew. If this opportunity is lost there will eventually be a mutually destructive war that no one will win – the Lebanon war proved that Israel must now confront the fact that its neighbors are becoming its military equals and US aid cannot save it. Indeed, America's free gifts enabled Israel to start a war in July 2006 with illusions identical to those that also caused the Bush Administration to embark on its Iraq folly.

Israel's power after 1947 was based on its military supremacy over its weaker neighbors. It is in the process of losing this dominance – if it has not already. Lesser problems, mainly demographic, will only be aggravated if tension persists. It simply cannot survive being allied with the United States, because the Americans will either leave the region or embark on a war that threatens Israel's very existence. It is time for Israel to become "normal" and make peace with its neighbors, but that will require it to make major concessions. It can do that if it embarks upon an independent foreign policy, which it can immediately undertake in relation to Syria.

5

The United States and War with Iran

The Middle East problem, as I stated in the Introduction, is the consequence of the unrealistic division of the Ottoman Empire after World War I, and Iran's present crisis began – for contemporary purposes – with the British and American overthrow of Mohammed Mossadegh in 1954. And because both Israel and the rest of the modern Middle East are a legacy of World War I's impact on the region, there is a great and unavoidable overlap of these topics.

As a consequence of the US invasion of Iraq, Iran now has America to thank, at least in large part, for its greatly increased oil revenues, giving it the resources adequate to resist American hostility, invest huge sums in the Gulf nations, and buy Russian equipment capable of shooting down any nation's planes. Instead of making Iraq safe for the oil companies and milking its riches, the US managed to make Iran far more powerful strategically and economically. In the process of invading Iraq, the US has lost a great deal of influence in the entire region because the Persian Gulf states possess an enormous amount of American dollars – the currency in which petroleum is priced. In March 2008, when Secretary of State Rice went to the Gulf region, the Saudis,

Jordanians, and Egyptians informed her they could not support more American adventures with Iran. They also told her that the US was creating an impossible, chaotic mess in Iraq, thereby destabilizing the entire region. President Bush's visit to Israel, Saudi Arabia, and Egypt in late May 2008 consisted of a love feast with the Jewish state and a didactic lecture to the Arabs. Never has the US been so hopelessly out of tune with the Arab world. Since at least 1945, never has its influence there been weaker.

Iran, meanwhile, has emerged strategically dominant in the region and is using its immense oil revenues to build its influence in every direction. It possesses the second largest petroleum reserve in the world and has successfully resisted all American efforts to isolate it. Petroleum in all forms is one of those raw materials that possess a transcendent value regardless of price. Without energy an economy has no power, and without power it will be primitive. Iran is simply the wrong nation for the US to challenge.

Iran can also ignite the Shiite majority in the Middle East to come to its aid. The events in Lebanon in May 2008, when Bush was touring the region, indicated that war against Iran also means wars wherever there are Shiites.

Nothing quite illustrates the end of American power so well as its strategy in the Middle East – where it has sustained Israel, made war in Iraq, and tried several times since 1954 (successfully in that case) to overthrow Teheran governments. Its numerous interventions in the region, from their inception, have produced contradictions and chaos. The US wars in Iraq and Afghanistan have meant the "war on terror" has simply moved to Pakistan – a nation that has nuclear weapons, the means to deliver them, and a highly unstable politics. Indeed, the US has already tried – unsuccessfully as of this moment

– to control entirely Pakistan's nuclear bombs. The net effect of America's efforts has been to spread the conflict to places it has an even more remote chance of success. It has refused to acknowledge the futility of its efforts. Indeed, it is at the time of this writing confronting Pakistan with demands that may yet lead to more futile adventures. Failure is now producing more failure as American foreign policy reaches a cul-de-sac.

ISRAEL, IRAN, AND THE BUSH ADMINISTRATION
(Counterpunch, February 10/11, 2007, revised May 2008)

There has been a qualitative leap in military technology that makes all inherited conventional wisdom, and war as an instrument of political policy, utterly irrelevant, not just to the United States but to any other state that embarks upon it. Nations should have realized this a century ago, but they did not. But there have been decisive changes in balances of power, and more accurate and destructive weapons – and soon nuclear bombs and the missiles to deliver them – are becoming increasingly available to poorer countries. Technology is moving much more rapidly than the diplomatic and political resources or will to control its inevitable consequences.

The United States should have learned its lesson in Vietnam, and its public is aware of that to a far greater extent than its politicians. (As of April 2008, nearly two-thirds of Americans – as opposed to 23 percent when the war began in March 2003 – thought it was a mistake to send troops to Iraq, making it at least as unpopular as the Vietnam War.) The war in Iraq has also reaffirmed the decisive limits of technology when fighting against enemies who are decentralized and determined. It has been extraordinarily expensive but militarily ineffective, and America is ineluctably losing its vast undertaking. Rivals are much more equal, and wars are more protracted and expensive for those who persist in fighting them. America's hegemonic ambitions throughout the globe can now be more successfully challenged.

The ultramodern Israel Defense Forces finally realized this in Lebanon in July 2006, when Hizbollah rockets destroyed or seriously damaged at least 20 of their best tanks and they were fought to a draw – abandoning the field of battle and losing their precious aura of invincibility. Growing demoralization well before the Lebanon war plagued Israel, and the percentage of Jews with higher academic degrees who migrated grew steadily after 2002. Israel exports brain power to an extent very high by world standards. The Lebanon war and talk of "existential" threats to the state's very existence – from both Israeli and, allegedly, Iranian leaders – only served to aggravate this defeatism and the desire to leave. At the end of January, 78 percent of Israelis were "unhappy" with their leaders for a variety of reasons.

Israeli politics has always been highly unstable by any standard, but the corruption and other scandals that are now plaguing it exceed any in its history, paralleling its loss of confidence in its military power. Alienation from the political class in Israel has never been greater, and Prime Minister Ehud Olmert and his cronies hope that spreading fear of an Iranian nuclear bomb will help them ride out a political storm that has seen his poll-rating plummet to a record low. But fear works both ways, frightening away the people who can emigrate most easily and keeping out tourists and foreign investors.

Moreover, the Israeli public's anxiety has not been allayed by reports of the efficacy of the anti-missile systems Israel has installed at great expense. The Iranians have mastered all of the technical basics of missile technology, according to Israeli experts, and although the quality and precision of Iran's missiles may leave something to be desired, they can inflict immense damage. Israeli specialists argue that the missile defense shield Israel possesses – in common with those of all other nations – is not sufficient to protect it. Syria has missiles also – not so effective as the Iranian ones, but much closer and likewise capable of inflicting much damage.

Notwithstanding the apocalyptic proclamations on Iran's imminent nuclear power status by Olmert's major rival, Benjamin Netanyahu, or by the prime minister himself and some of his cabinet on occasions, this hysteria is politically motivated and intended to garner public support. Meir Dagan, the head of Mossad, told the Israeli Knesset in December 2006 that diplomatic efforts were "far from being over" – and that an Iranian nuclear bomb was at least two years or more off. Many Israeli strategists, including Yuval Diskin, head of Shin Bet, now regard Bush's war in Iraq as a highly destabilizing disaster for the entire region and a major boon to Iran's power, and they regret having endorsed it. A war with Iran would be far more dangerous. Worse yet, efforts to demonize Iran have failed. Only 36 percent of the Jewish population of Israel polled in January 2007 thought an Iranian nuclear attack the "biggest threat" to Israel.

Serious Israeli strategists overwhelmingly believe, to cite Reuven Pedatzur in *Ha'aretz* last November, that "mutual assured deterrence can be forged, with a high degree of success, between Israel and Iran." Israeli strategic thinking is highly realistic. Early this February a study released at a conference by the Institute for National Security Studies at Tel Aviv University predicted that Iran would behave rationally with nuclear weapons and "that the elimination of Israel is not considered to be an essential national interest" for it. Iran "will act logically, evaluating the price and risks involved." A preemptive attack on Iran's nuclear research sites would "be a strategic mistake," Pedatzur warned the conference, and the use of tactical nuclear weapons against them sheer folly. "Our best option is open nuclear deterrence."

Israeli experts have come to the realization that US policy in the Middle East is not merely an immense failure but also decisively inhibits Israel reorienting its foreign policy to confront the realities of the region that the Jews have chosen to live in.

Peace ... or War

The only security Israel can have will be a result of its signing peace accords with the Palestinians and the neighboring countries. It is no more likely than the US to defeat its enemies on the field of battle, and its arms have in effect been neutralized. The war in Lebanon was only an augury of the decisive limits of its military power. It is in this context that secret Israeli talks with Syria have enormous significance. They began in January 2004 in Turkey with the approval of Sharon, moving on to Switzerland, where the Swiss Foreign Office played the role of intermediary. By August 2005 they had become very broad-based, covering territorial, water, border, and political questions. Details remained to be ironed out, but the talks were a quantum leap toward solving one of the region's crucial problems. When the Baker–Hamilton Study Group filed its recommendations in December 2006, negotiations with Syria were especially stressed – a point Baker reiterated when he testified to the US Senate Committee on Foreign Relations on January 30, 2007. Baker undoubtedly knew about the secret talks and Syria's explicit statements that it wished to break with radical Islamic movements and was ready to discuss its ties with Iran, Hizbollah, and Hamas.

These nominally secret talks were made public on January 8, 2007, when Egyptian President Hosni Mubarak accused the United States in an interview with an Israeli paper of obstructing peace between Israel and Syria. *Ha'aretz*'s Akiva Eldar then published a series of extremely detailed accounts, including the draft accord, confirming that Syria offered a far-reaching and equitable peace treaty that would provide for Israel's security and is comprehensive – and which would divorce Syria from Iran and even create a crucial distance between it and Hizbollah and Hamas. The Bush Administration's role in scuttling any peace accord was decisive. C. David Welch, Assistant Secretary of State for Near Eastern Affairs, sat in at the final meeting, and two former senior CIA officials were present in all of the meetings and sent regular reports to Vice-President Dick Cheney's office. The press has been full of details on how the American role was decisive, because it has war, not peace, at the top of its agenda.

Most of the Israeli establishment favored an accord with Syria. On January 28, important Israelis met publicly in Jaffa and called the Israeli response "an irresponsible gamble with the State of Israel" since it made Cheney arbiter of Israeli national interests. They included former IDF chief of staff Amnon Lipkin Shahak, former Shin Bet chief Ya'akov Perry, former directors of the Foreign Ministry David Kimche and Alon Liel (who negotiated the deal and believes it is very serious), and the like. Shlomo Ben-Ami, former foreign minister, has since supported their position and argued that it is "too important" for Israel to endorse yet "another failure in the US strategy."

But Olmert has explicitly said that the Bush Administration opposes a negotiated peace with Syria. Therefore, he is opposed to it also. Olmert's contradiction is that he wants to remain closely allied to the US, whatever its policies, yet he is now one of the most unpopular prime ministers in Israel's history and in power only because of Sharon's stroke. Israel is a crucial pillar of American policy in the entire region, but this policy is failing. An alliance with America is Olmert's recipe for political defeat when the inevitable election is called. That is his problem.

WILL THE US ATTACK IRAN?
(Antiwar.blog, October 1, 2007, revised May 2008)

The US and European economies are now in a crisis, and it may be protracted. The dollar is falling in value, Gulf States and others may abandon it. A war with Iran would produce economic chaos, because oil would be even more expensive, becoming so scarce for the masses that political instability would ensue in countless countries. There are states ready to sell oil, such as Russia and Venezuela, who are already at maximum production and becoming richer thereby. America's strategy in Latin America and Europe is in a shambles. In a word, the balance of world economic power and the role of nations that Washington now considers adversaries is involved, and these are great issues.

The Gulf States do not like Shiite Iran, but they are dependent on peace, not war, and Iran is investing immense sums in their economies. The combined gross domestic product of the nations in the Gulf Co-operation Council, measured in US dollars, has more than doubled from 2002 to 2007, allowing them to embark on a campaign to build skyscrapers and exotic buildings. Awash with money, the Gulf States are being asked by major American banks to bail them out of their follies over the past decade. Many are abandoning the US dollar as a reserve currency – or are in the process of doing so – because their food imports are rising and the value of the dollar is falling. The Gulf States are losing vast sums thereby. If asked, they are extremely unlikely to grant US planes or missiles overflight permission. Iran will always exist in the region and the Gulf States must live with it. They increasingly want to and wish the United States would cease trying to change reality.

The Saudis are the last bastion of American power in the region but they too are losing vast sums and wobbling. Rice's visit in March 2008 was a total failure and she was told to expect no cooperation. For good reason, there are important Israeli strategists who fear that the Palestine question will ultimately be decided by the immense revenues the anti-Israel Arab states receive from oil. The roles these states can play is endless – the "oil weapon" and revenue can be decisive.

The US public and Congress are variable factors, although a growing and large majority have turned against the Iraq War – as they eventually did on Vietnam – and increasingly want negotiations rather than conflict with Iran. As the last election proved, anyone who thinks the Democrats will stop wars is fooling him- or herself. But war with Iran would require new authorizations. Then Congress would, potentially, be very important.

Cheney and the neocons are very articulate ideologues, but will they volunteer to fight Iran, and if so what will they do on the battlefield? How many effective fighters do they have at the *Weekly Standard* or the American Enterprise Institute?

The US military is at the present moment overstretched. Its troops are marginalized cannon fodder, poorer men who are increasingly demoralized. It is losing both its wars in Iraq and Afghanistan. Everything is being sacrificed for these wars: money, equipment in Asia, American military power globally and, most important, control of the Western Hemisphere. Most of the members of the Joint Chiefs of Staff oppose a war with Iran. According to an article in *Salon* (September 28, 2007), "the military would revolt and there would be no pilots to fly those missions" were it ordered to go to war against Iran. Without them, there is no danger. Military analysts and writers influential in the Pentagon deem war with Iran the height of folly – a view shared by most American officers. Some senior military commanders have threatened to resign if ordered to make war against Iran. The Afghan war crossed the border into the northern tribal areas of Pakistan many years ago, and is becoming far more intense after the US almost defeated the Taliban. American troops are being moved from Iraq to Afghanistan, where the conflict may now last for years. The US simply does not have the manpower to fight Iran while resources are tied up in another country, whether in South Asia or a nation elsewhere in the so-called Third World.

"Bunker busters" can only knock out so many bunkers – but not all. If such bombs are nuclear they may be very useful, but they are also radioactive. In addition to killing enemies, they may kill friends and nearby US soldiers also. It depends on where you drop them and the wind.

What will 65 million Iranians do, and what sort of technology do they possess? In addition to its known purchases of arms from Russia, Iran has been on the open market and possesses weapons and technology the US knows nothing about. Iran fought against Iraq for about a decade, and suffered around half a million casualties. In 2008 it had over 15 million men fit for military service, and 15 million women. Perhaps Iran will roll over, but it's not likely. There are a number of tiny islands in the Gulf it has had years to fortify. Can 90 percent of their weapons be knocked out? Even the remainder will be sufficient to sink many boats and tankers. Iran has indigenously-built unmanned aerial vehicles (UAV) that can penetrate US carrier group air defenses. In mid 2007 the US navy had nearly half of its 277 warships in or near Iran, all confined to a small area. Iran had 140 surface boats and six subs. In the event of war with Iran, the oil exported through the Gulf would thereby be reduced, and perhaps cease altogether. Then, too, American soldiers in Iraq would be hostage to Iranian recriminations, at least by arming their Shiite allies.

Iran is now selling about 2.5 million barrels of oil a day to Japan, China, and many American allies, and building ever-larger foreign exchange reserves, with which it is buying the most advanced Russian military equipment capable of bringing down airplanes and sinking US boats effectively. Russia and Iran are now much closer and increasingly collaborate on energy policy – making Iran a far more difficult nation to confront blithely. Given this prosperity, American economic sanctions are not bringing Iran to its knees. Whatever problems Iran has internally, it has more than enough coherence within the nation to defeat the American military colossus. The US lost a simulated August 2002 war game with Iran. And it would lose again today because the Iranian military has become far more potent.

Israel may be a factor. Olmert and his cronies are doing their utmost to give the United States a pretext for war with

Iran. But Israeli planes must cross Syrian and Jordanian air space, and the Iranians will be prepared for any that are not shot down over Syria. Israeli counter-measures may be effective, but may not. Hence a number of Israeli pilots will realize they are embarking on suicide missions.

If Israel uses its nuclear weapons they may destroy many, even all, Iranian targets, but they will also create fallout that will kill friends as well as foes. But unless it uses them it lacks the aviation resources to stop the Iranian bomb program permanently. And the Arab world will overcome its natural fractiousness and unify as never before. A protracted, decentralized war would very likely follow, its exact form a mystery but an immense risk. Scarcely any American administration would agree to Israel employing its nuclear weapons.

Iran is likely to get nuclear bombs sooner or later. So will many other nations. The Arab states in the Middle East are developing nuclear power for nominally peaceful purposes but some may build nuclear bombs also. The Saudis tried to buy nuclear bombs from Pakistan in 1988 and very likely have nuclear weapons already – to fight Iran, Israel, or both. Israel has hundreds. At least some Israeli strategists believe deterrence works. Why risk war? There may be other factors. The US effort to impose a commercial and economic boycott on Iran is, at best, working unevenly. Perhaps it is failing altogether.

The Bush–Cheney Administration, as the Iraq War proved, is full of irrational people, and there is no way to account for them. Olmert and Defense Minister Ehud Barak want to give the US a pretext for, and indeed want to trap the US into, a war that is far more dangerous than the war against Iraq. It is a war that may lead to Israel's destruction. Cheney and his underlings were eager for war with Iraq – and only as the beginning of a much vaster war against Syria, Iran, and even other nations – but the world economic crisis is working against them. But not everyone in Washington thinks like them, especially in the military, and those on Wall Street who have the most to lose from a war have great political influence. We are obliged to count on them because that is the way the US has operated for decades.

Most of the wars the US has fought it has lost. It would be very likely to lose a protracted war with Iran, if it decides to fight. But it probably will not.

6
The Limits of Intelligence

I have always been interested in the limits of intelligence, limits that reappear in numerous cases wherever American foreign policy is pursued. The following essay, slightly revised, explores a crucial example, but one can study the Korean War or those in Central and South America and come to the same conclusion: US foreign policy has always suffered from a fatal disjunction between policy and reality. And it has suffered countless defeats – which have increased in frequency – because of these illusions. In an essay I wrote for *Science & Society* in the summer of 1980 I argued that it was also a myth to assume that intelligence and rationality guided the administration and reform of the American economy in the twentieth century.

The problem, essentially, is that the American system is not rational and predictable. It is incapable of being implemented rationally because its goals far exceed its resources. The US is hardly alone in suffering a myopia regarding reality – it is the hallmark of history since time immemorial. World War I was begun by nations that had fatal illusions, transforming all of subsequent history. What this general attribute of all-powerful nations proves is that theories which assume rationality and predictability – the coherence theories of Max

Weber, theories of the Enlightenment and progress, and other theories assuming that human and institutional behavior is orderly and logical – are quite irrelevant to the course of reality. American power is but the latest example. Earlier there were imperial ambitions of the Spanish, the British, the French.... All failed because of their numerous contradictions. Illusions about reality formed part of these contradictions, and that is the topic of this essay.

In the case of the US, what passes as strategy in official circles is far less the result of reflection than of the major military services – the army, navy, and air force – seeking to get a larger share of the Defense budget at the expense of each other. Dangers were concocted with this solely in mind, and the one thing such a process is not is rational. The air force must have dangers of a certain sort, the navy yet another, and they have each manufactured evils to justify their budget allocation rather than to assess reality objectively. The dangers the Soviet Union presented were very often, perhaps always, the result of such struggles between competing military services. The White House had to adjudicate these differences in relation to the larger goals it perceived as essential. Presidents often used service rivalries as excuses for adopting their favored policies; but these rivalries were always a factor of consequence in the entire intelligence process.

In *After Socialism* I detailed the faults and limits of all systematic theories. The power of reason is a subtle, attractive siren song and it has suffused all social theories since the eighteenth century. Notwithstanding the germ of validity in some of them, it is the limits of such systems that are more crucial, and which appear in the conduct of political, economic, and foreign policies of many nations. Illusions are here much more common than a candid confrontation with reality. American foreign policy is but one of many examples.

On the whole, I have argued, there is a theoretical void in many domains of social science, and the real system consists of the sum of its parts. There is power and the myths sustaining it: of the market, of infallible leaders claiming heavenly sanction or the attribute of profound insight that makes them qualified to lead. But there is far too much incoherence in the behavior of nations, their leaders, and their institutions to formulate systematic, predictable ideas. This is true of societies or leaders generally, whether they call themselves capitalist, socialist, holy, or whatever.

In the case of the United States, the way it treats fictions as facts – and why – has been crucial in shaping the demise of its immense power.

THE LIMITS OF INTELLIGENCE:
THE COLD WAR, VIETNAM, AND IRAQ
(From an essay published in Lloyd C. Gardner and Marilyn Young, eds., *Iraq and the Lessons of Vietnam*, New York: The New Press, 2007, revised May 2008)

Crises, imminent dangers, and threats to the nation's security and vital interests have been intrinsic to American foreign policy since at least 1947. They have mobilized a reticent public and, even more important, a Congress that must perpetually approve huge sums to implement its military dimensions. In this context, there is scant regard for reality and images of perils are of the essence. Indeed, political leaders themselves often come to believe illusions as the facts fall by the wayside. Deliberate exaggerations, if not outright falsehoods, have been routine since President Harry S. Truman enunciated his classic Doctrine in March 1947. The only way he could convince a budget-minded Congress and indifferent public to accept his quite limited but costly program was to paint the crisis in Greece and Turkey in the most foreboding global terms. Congress and the American public are "not sufficiently aware," as Undersecretary of State Dean Acheson put it, of the need to spend the money essential for what was seen as a protracted crisis encompassing all Europe and even much of the world. George Kennan, the key theoretician on containing Soviet power whose ideas had immense influence, objected to the Truman Doctrine's strident tone, and even Secretary of State George C. Marshall thought the President was overstating the case. Exaggeration and the threat of nefarious dangers became intrinsic to how Washington portrayed the world after 1947 and it continues until this day despite the disappearance of the Soviet bloc.[1] It encourages Congress to produce funds that might otherwise not be available.

From 1947 onward – in the words of Willard C. Matthias, who was for many years in charge of the CIA's Soviet estimates and retired in 1973 as a senior official – "there developed a four-decade-long debate between the civilian and military intelligence agencies over Soviet intentions."[2] Massive arms spending was dependent on portraying the USSR's goals in the most ominous ways possible, which meant emphasizing Soviet capabilities rather than intentions, and ignoring their inherently cautious, fatalist but passive Marxist view of change and the historical process. Liberalizing tendencies in the USSR were dismissed, the gravity of the Soviet–Chinese schism was grossly underestimated, and, as Matthias states it, "after 1968, our rational and balanced approach to making

judgments about the Soviets came under increasing attack."[3]
Needless to say, diplomatic exchanges with the Russians were
frowned upon even at crucial moments of the Korean War,
and negotiations were considered a last resort only.

The war in Vietnam, but also most other aspects of
American foreign and military policy since 1946, must be
assessed in this context. President Richard Nixon had a deep
antipathy to the CIA, one that Henry Kissinger and Secretary
of Defense Melvin Laird shared, and he fired Richard Helms
in 1973 as director of the CIA because he refused to allow
the Agency to serve as a cover for the Watergate break-in.
President Jimmy Carter's chief aides regarded its estimates
as a "nuisance," not so much inaccurate as "irrelevant."[4]
Ronald Reagan appointed William Casey head of the CIA
in 1981, and Casey – as one of his successors reports it
– "argued, he fought, he yelled, he grumped..." with his
analysts and only more roughly continued what was in fact
a decades-old policy.[5] He pursued his own foreign policy
agenda aggressively and maintained that "Our estimating
program has become a powerful instrument in forcing the
pace in the policy area."[6] No one in 1989, the CIA included,
had any foreboding whatsoever of the total collapse in the
Soviet bloc, with its immense consequences.

Such a critical assessment of the role that objective
intelligence played in the decision-making process is no
longer the opinion of dissident historians but virtually the
consensus position in memoirs written by former intelligence
officials. Notwithstanding many very able people in the CIA,
and their access to a tremendous amount of information,
since 1946 there has never been an objective, disinterested
intelligence system that shaped policy. Preconceived ideas or
interests determined how the world was portrayed, and the

outcome was disastrous if only because action frequently bore little relation to reality. Even more unforgivable from the government's perspective, these illusions and misconceptions often produced grave failures.

The distortion of information for political objectives became worse with time, but it preceded the Vietnam War by well over a decade and simply continues in our own day. The CIA, which often produced excellent analytic assessments, was taken seriously only insofar as its burgeoning action wing could implement foreign policies covertly. The Vietnam War evolved in this context and such erroneous and often duplicitous estimates have provided the setting of every crisis since then – Iraq included. It is crucial that we regard the intelligence and information process as inherently polluted, subject to political whims. The problem has never been one of knowledge but of policy.

The American government had capable people working on Vietnam and they knew much about that nation. George W. Allen joined the Pentagon's intelligence service in 1949 and immediately became involved with France's effort to retain its Indochina colonies; his memoir is required reading on the entire Vietnam experience. In 1963, scandalized by the American military's myopia and mores, he moved to the CIA and soon became its leading Vietnam analyst. He met innumerable decision-makers in this capacity. When he retired from the CIA in 1979 he worked for them on contract for the next 15 years and the CIA cleared his book. In it he confirms how crucial decisions were based on illusions and falsehoods.

Allen recounts how Eisenhower and Dulles strongly opposed France following what the Americans were then doing in Korea – signing a ceasefire agreement and making a settlement with their enemies after being stalemated on the battlefield. They wanted the French to fight harder and longer, which France refused to do. The US opposed the Geneva Accords and, "basing their views on a set of assumptions that we believed were entirely unrealistic," it foredoomed the French mission in Indochina.[7] The Eisenhower Administration prevented the Geneva Accords' conditions on reunification elections from being implemented and violated its military provisions. The history of the rest of the decade is well known, but every step of the way CIA analysts accurately predicted what would go wrong.

The so-called Tonkin Gulf crisis of August 1964 "astonished" Allen because he was aware that covert Saigon and American missions were taking place in the Gulf and that the North Vietnamese would investigate them. At first he thought that a branch of the American military did not know what another section was up to, "but I did not realize how eagerly the administration was seeking a pretext for a major escalation" in the hope of shoring up the Saigon regime. The same was true of the Pleiku incidents of early 1965, which became an excuse for "a retaliation waiting for something to happen; the Pleiku attacks were a convenient trigger for intended escalation." It was a justification for permanently bombing North Vietnam.[8]

Robert L. Sansom and Jeffrey Race both studied the land and peasant question in Vietnam for the American government and published insightful books well before the war ended. Both asserted that land reform was a key precondition of a successful anti-communist political mobilization in the South, and both were ignored. Race describes how Washington's "policy was founded on and protected by deception and outrageous lies," and how a general told him that to identify America's errors in Vietnam was off bounds and the Pentagon "cannot permit such subjects to be discussed." That there were structural reasons for peasant support of the communists "simply couldn't get through" to the men at the top.[9] There were also articulate skeptics within the Pentagon who thought the war was futile, and its Systems Analysis Office published a very informative report every six weeks or so; the Joint Chiefs of Staff several times sought to close down or restrict it. Many critics of the war worked at the Rand Corporation, and Rand employees leaked The Pentagon Papers. There was, in short, plenty of accurate information available – for those who wanted to read and use it. But it simply made no difference because the vast gap between reality and policy was unbridgeable.

In 1998 the CIA released Harold P. Ford's detailed account of the period 1962–68, which complements and corroborates Allen's memoir.[10] Ford makes it perfectly clear that Secretary of Defense Robert McNamara's later complaint that there were no "Vietnam experts" to whom he could turn is simply false. He refused to heed their advice whenever they warned against the series of disasters that Allen and others describe. Among the many failures were the American inability to understand communist military doctrine or estimate accurately the strength of communist forces – the "order-of-battle" which became a contention between the CIA and Pentagon. In addition, the Johnson Administration unconditionally supported the venal and corrupt Nguyen Van Thieu becoming a virtual dictator, thereby ending the chronic political instability that followed the American-endorsed assassination of Ngo Dinh Diem. The level of corruption that permeated Thieu's entire system, from the state to the army, was well known and tolerated in Washington; Allen provides additional details. And all Washington administrations trained and equipped the

Saigon army to fight conventional war according to official American doctrine. It was, of course, mainly a guerilla war.

The myths of progress in the war were conscious falsehoods intended to manipulate public opinion and justify the futile endeavor. When Allen and other CIA analysts objected they were told to conform. In numerous instances American officials consciously issued erroneous data, such as the hamlet evaluation statistics. At no time was truth given a higher priority than political convenience or the lies both the politicians and generals propounded. The military intelligence and CIA were constantly struggling with each other for analytic domination, and the CIA lost most of these bureaucratic turf wars. And while some politicians, military, and CIA action people – those whose hawkish policies were already predetermined – deluded themselves and undoubtedly really believed these fairy tales, most knew that their careers depended on them being optimists.

The most serious consequence of these deceptions was the so-called order-of-battle controversy before the Tet Offensive in February 1968. The lower the numbers of communist forces the more progress the US military could claim, and so they refused to count the various local forces – roughly 300,000 men disappeared because admitting their existence, General Creighton Abrams argued in August 1967, would produce a "gloomy" conclusion.[11]

The CIA objected up to a point, but eventually had to accept the distortions; both Allen and Ford are very detailed on this particular controversy. Ultimately, General William Westmoreland unsuccessfully sued CBS for allowing a leading CIA specialist on the order-of-battle to expound his views. But the communists during the Tet Offensive had far larger military forces than most American officials believed and their stunning attacks changed American politicians' and, even more ominously, public perceptions of reality. The Tet defeat, Allen insists, was all the greater because of the "overblown psychological campaign in the fall of 1967," which was also essential for Lyndon Johnson's reelection ambitions.[12] The falsified data, in the end, was believed by those seeking initially to manipulate public opinion, and the Tet defeat was the beginning of the end for the protracted American effort to win the Vietnam War.

Lies became the rule. The public had to be led along and, as Allen recounts, "On many occasions the truth was grotesquely and deliberately distorted in order to make a point."[13] But Vietnam was only one of many examples of how foreign policies were formulated: "our policies tend to be excessively dominated by aggressive individuals or organizations, or by the interplay of bureaucratic politics, rather than by rational deliberation of national interests."[14] After thirty-odd years in this role, Allen became disillusioned.

Both Ford and Allen come to the same conclusion, to cite Allen, "that our leaders tended toward self-delusion."[15] What is most significant in both of the Allen and Ford accounts is that men with first-hand knowledge wrote them; McGeorge Bundy emerges as a villain and cynical manipulator, and Robert McNamara as a pathetic character, confused but committed to the war. Critical historians had reached this conclusion long before. But what is unique is Allen's intimate account of meetings and confrontations, revealing the mindset of men hell-bent on the path of destruction and victory.

The CIA has produced many unhappy people who had access to much more information than did policy critics and who came to identical conclusions as them. Technology over the past 15 years has vastly increased the volume of information available to the intelligence community, making research and analysis more rather than less difficult – and more liable to be irrelevant or wrong. Anyone who reads the CIA's unclassified version of *Studies in Intelligence* knows that there are a significant number of analysts who are quite candid, suggesting that "much of the information" the CIA gets, "to be blunt, is garbage."[16] Other memoirs, dealing with the CIA's action section or the Pentagon's special operations forces, describe endless ineptitude and confusion. Screwing up covert efforts is so common that it is practically the rule rather than the exception. But it was not only covert operations that failed. Confusion was inherent in the competing services' refusal since 1947 to subordinate their rival fiefdoms by standardizing technical communication systems and sharing basic intelligence, a deficiency that has increased with time and today plagues the American military more than ever.[17]

Publicly, the CIA defended its reputation for gathering intelligence expertly and impersonally until the mid 1970s House and Senate investigations. Before then, its critics confirmed its failures mainly by deduction, but the Congressional investigations portrayed an organization that was not merely malevolent but also simply incompetent on many critical matters. It did not anticipate the Korean War, the Czech crisis of 1968, the October 1973 Middle East War, the 1974 Portuguese upheaval, India's explosion of a nuclear device in 1972, the fall of the Shah in 1979 – and much else that subsequently took the US by surprise. That policy predilection determines what its analysts report, or that the CIA's directors have been ambitious careerists who often tailor their reporting, has been conventional wisdom for decades, and what has occurred in the case of Iraq was only the rule. Biases and political interests and ambitions, especially reelection, have made policy-makers reluctant to accept intelligence they do not wish to hear – and most senior intelligence officials acknowledge these constraints. Those who make decisions want intelligence to support their goals, and if it does not then they use it selectively or ignore it entirely because they have both confidence in their own judgments and their own agendas. Very few senior intelligence officials believe that their objectivity will prevent bad or dangerous policies from being pursued. As one of them put it: "But the idea that intelligence can ignore the political atmosphere in which it is being delivered is, again, a Panglossian affliction."[18]

The Case of Iraq

There are great cultural, political, and physical differences between Vietnam and Iraq that cannot be minimized, and the geopolitical situation is entirely different. After all, the US encouraged and materially supported Saddam Hussein in his war with Iran throughout the 1980s because it feared a militantly Shiite Iran would dominate the Persian Gulf region. It still does fear this, and if the Shiite majority takes over the Iraqi government or if the federalism written into the new Iraqi constitution leads to a real or de facto partition of the country, one or the other of which is very probable, Iran is more likely than ever to attain its geopolitical ambitions – thereby dominating the entire region. But putting this fundamental paradox in the American position aside, which makes the transfer of power to the Iraqi Shiites and real democracy highly unlikely, the US has ignored the lessons of the traumatic Vietnam experience and is today repeating many of the errors that produced defeat there. By April 2008 – five years after the Iraq War began – a report issued by the

National Defense University, the Pentagon's elite educational institution, concluded that the war was "a major debacle," likely to be lost.

The intelligence process worked badly in both Vietnam and Iraq. Policy always precedes this process and definitively shapes the outcome, but precisely because both wars ended in failures we know much more about what intelligence said – in part because whistleblowers have much more incentive to reveal the truth. In September 1991, Scott Ritter, who had previously been an officer in US Marine intelligence, went to work for the United Nations' weapons inspection team charged with the task of confirming whether Iraq retained weapons of mass destruction (WMD) or the means of delivering them. American, British, and Israeli intelligence fed him their best information. Early in his mission, which involved frequent inspections of sites the UN chose, he concluded that Iraq had complied with UN disarmament criteria, which the defection in August 1995 of Hussein Kamal, Saddam Hussein's son-in-law, only confirmed. Still, every American administration from 1991 onward maintained the myth of Iraqi possession of WMD because their real goal, Ritter concluded, was regime change.[19] As for ties between al-Qaeda and Saddam's regime, and the latter teaching the former how to use WMD (which Bush gave as a reason for the war), from the end of September 2001 onward the President knew that the secular Iraq regime was hostile to bin Laden's Islamic fanaticism. Well before the war began, the US Defense Intelligence Agency identified the source of this allegation as a fabricator. The CIA – much to the irritation of the Bush Administration, and especially Vice-President Richard Cheney and Defense Secretary Donald Rumsfeld – provided a great deal of evidence to prove that war was avoidable.[20] The real reasons for the US embarking on war in Iraq lie elsewhere, and assigning a precise weight to them is a dubious task. Crucial, however, was a mentality, which Rumsfeld expressed to the President-elect, that the new administration should be "forward-leaning" in its foreign policy and end the Clinton Administration's purported defensiveness.[21] Bush, of course, was of the same mind. Intelligence was never important in defining action, and the Bush Administration not only ignored it but – as the Valerie Plame case revealed – often consciously distorted what the intelligence community was reporting.

The resemblance to Vietnam is remarkable, but only because all of the important US foreign policies have been handled in a similar manner. What was crucial was that the Bush Administration resolved before it took office to be aggressive, just as John F. Kennedy and Lyndon Johnson had done in the 1960s, although it was unclear in what region of the world they would concentrate their operations. In both Vietnam and Iraq, unexpected defeats and surprises awaited the US just as they awaited every nation that embarked on wars over the past two centuries.

What followed thereafter in the run-up to the Iraq War was perfectly predictable. Detailed reports from many sources, such as Ritter, the CIA itself, or experts on Iraqi arms and politics, were essentially discarded in favor of exceedingly dubious but convenient information, the most bizarre and unreliable of which came from "Curveball," an Iraqi whom German intelligence considered wholly untrustworthy and whose veracity only Ahmad Chalabi's network had vouched for. The CIA issued fabricator warnings on some of these people and never believed them. A year before the invasion, most of the intelligence community agreed that reports that Saddam Hussein was attempting to import uranium were false, but Bush ignored them and often cited such fictions to justify invading Iraq. Whatever the CIA's director might have said to the President, and for whatever reasons, the large majority of the CIA knew that Iraq had long ceased trying to develop nuclear weapons and most opposed embarking on war there.[22] Other official experts emphatically cautioned decision-makers about the chaotic future of a post-Saddam Iraq and the threat of civil war and they were also ignored. For public purposes the CIA was purportedly the main source of the utter falsehoods the Bush Administration used to justify going to war in Iraq when in fact the Agency warned it had strong doubts about them.[23] The Administration had no scruples whatsoever in doing this, and it was only following many deep-rooted precedents: Congress and the public are told whatever will win their acquiescence. But such efforts work for a limited time only.

In both Vietnam and Iraq successive US administrations slighted the advice of the most knowledgeable intelligence experts. But America's leaders have repeatedly believed what they wanted, not what their intelligence told them. Cynicism and a contempt for the public often exists among those who covet and gain power. The extent to which self-delusion and political convenience become intertwined can be endlessly debated, and elements of both can be found in countless cases. While it is an issue that cannot be resolved definitively, and every case and individual is different, such devious procedures greatly subverted the rationality – and prudence – that intelligence is supposed to provide.

But there can be no doubt that the Pentagon in the 1960s had an uncritical faith in its overwhelming firepower, its high technology, mobility, and mastery of the skies. This was a natural and timeless trait inherent in American mores, one that weapons producers have always reinforced. Social and political challenges, Washington believed, would fall to the side once the enemy was quickly destroyed. It still has faith in weapons, and Defense Secretary Donald Rumsfeld believes the military has the technology to "shock and awe" all adversaries. But, as in Vietnam, technology has been exceedingly fallible in Iraq and logistics also became even more of a nightmare because no ports exist close to many areas of conflict. Indeed, precisely because it had become infinitely more complicated, technology in Iraq failed even more quickly, while crucial and obvious problems, like the immense water deficit, proved surprisingly time-consuming and very expensive to deal with.[24]

Both the Vietnam and Iraq wars were exceedingly costly, in part because of the reliance on the latest technology and massive firepower as well as on incompetent and corrupt proxies. The Vietnam War was far more expensive than anticipated; it lasted much longer than predicted, and Johnson had to abandon much of his domestic program to pay for it. It was a major cause of the weakening of the dollar and the US ultimately going off the gold standard.[25] The war in Iraq has been very similar, also coming at the conjunction of massive budget deficits and a weakening dollar, greatly aggravating an unfavorable economic position. War in Iraq cost at least $439 billion by mid 2006, in three and one-half years exceeding well over half of what the Vietnam War cost over nine years, and estimates of its eventual long-term cost are nearly $3 trillion, making it the most expensive war in American history.

Wars in both Vietnam and Iraq were highly decentralized. When deployment reached a half-million American men in Vietnam the public turned against President Johnson and defeated his party. In the case of Iraq the public has become hostile to the adventure, if not anti-war, much more quickly; in late 2005 nearly two-thirds of the public disapproved of the President's handling of the situation in Iraq and 58 percent believed he has not given good reasons for keeping troops there. Fifty-seven percent believed he deliberately misled the people in order to make a case for war in Iraq. By February 2006, 63 percent of the American public thought the Iraq War was not worth the loss of American lives or the cost, and 48 percent favored immediate withdrawal. Bush's job approval rating kept on falling, hitting a low of 33 percent by the end of April 2006.[26] It has become consistently worse since then, revealing a mass political intelligence quite immune to manipulation by the press and media.

What happens in a nation's political, social, and economic spheres is far more decisive than military equations. That was the case in China in the late 1940s, in Vietnam in 1975, and it is also the case in Iraq today. Wars are ultimately won politically or not at all. This is true in every place and at all times. Leaders in Washington thought this interpretation of events in Vietnam was bizarre, and they ignored their experts whenever they frequently reminded them of the limits of military power. The importance of Vietnamese politics was slighted, escalations followed, and the "credibility" of American military power – the willingness to use it and win no matter how long it took or how much it cost – became the primary concern.

In both Vietnam and Iraq the public was mobilized on the basis of cynical falsehoods that ultimately backfired, causing a "credibility gap." People eventually ceased to believe anything Washington told them. Countless lies were told during the Vietnam War but eventually many of the men who counted most were themselves unable to separate truth from fiction. Most American leaders really believed that if the communists won in Vietnam the "dominoes" would fall and the Chinese would dominate all Southeast Asia. The Iraq War was initially justified because Saddam Hussein was purported to have weapons of mass destruction and ties to al-Qaeda; no evidence whatsoever for either allegation existed beforehand or has been found since.

There are about 160,000 American and foreign troops in Iraq (over 260,000 if support troops in the region are included) at the time of this writing – far more than Bush predicted would remain by this time – but, as in Vietnam, their morale is already low and sinking further. Bush's ratings have fallen dramatically as he has run up huge budget deficits and ignored domestic issues, such as health insurance, which greatly determine how people vote. He desperately needs many more soldiers in Iraq. Depending on the resistance or geopolitical context in the region, substantial numbers of American forces may remain in Iraq for many years. In Vietnam, President Nixon tried to "Vietnamize" the land war and transfer the burdens of soldiering to Nguyen Van Thieu's huge army. But its ranks were demoralized and Catholic-officered, and his army was organized entirely to maintain Thieu in power rather than win the victory that American forces could not attain.

The idea that the war can be "Iraqized" and that the local army will be loyal to America's nominal goals or be militarily effective is quixotic. As in Vietnam, where the Buddhists opposed the Catholic minority who comprised the leaders the US endorsed, Iraq is a nation divided ethnically and religiously, and Washington has the unenviable choice between the risks of disorder which its own lack of troops makes likely and civil war if it arms Iraqis. Elections have only exacerbated these differences greatly, not resolved them. The Shiites make up three-fifths of the Iraqi population, their leaders have their own political agendas, and their taking over of the army or the political regime will also strengthen Iran's influence and power in the region. Despite plenty of expert opinion to advise it, the Bush Administration has little perception of the complexity of the political problems it confronts in Iraq. All major Iraqi religious and ethnic groups have armed militias but US officials increasingly regard the Shiites as the greatest single threat to their authority. Afghanistan looms as a reminder of how military success depends ultimately on politics, and how things can go wrong.

"Iraqization" of the military conflict will not accomplish what has eluded the Americans, and in both Vietnam and Iraq the US underestimated the length of time it would have to remain and cultivated fatal illusions about the strength of its friends. While appraisals of the effectiveness or size of the Iraqi army vary, the US must prevent the Shiite majority who fill its ranks, many of whom are pro-Iranian, from becoming even more powerful. It is therefore now incorporating Sunni officers who worked for Saddam Hussein before the war, a total reversal of its policy when it began the conflict. The Bush Administration's reliance on local troops to fulfill US goals is an act of desperation, no more likely to be successful in Iraq than it was in Vietnam. Vietnam was a religiously divided nation but Iraq is even more disunited internally, and the possibility of civil war is greater. In Vietnam the communists rode to power by creating a nationalist resistance to the French and Americans, but in Iraq there is likely to be chaos. As in Vietnam, the US will lose the war in Iraq because all wars are decided by a larger social, political, and economic context which American military power has never been able to control or respond to.

Rumsfeld's admission in his confidential memo of October 2003 that "we lack the metrics to know if we are winning or losing the global war on terror" was an indication that key members of the Bush Administration were far less confident of what they are doing than they were when they embarked on war.[27] But as in Vietnam, when Defense Secretary Robert McNamara ceased to believe that victory was inevitable, it is too late to change course and now the credibility of America's military power is at stake. So too is the role that Iran will play as the dominant power in the region – one likely to be armed with nuclear weapons.

Eventually, domestic politics takes precedence over everything else. It did during the Vietnam War and it is very likely it will also be the case with the war in Iraq. By 1968 the polls were turning against the Democrats and the Tet Offensive in February caught President Johnson by surprise because he and his generals refused to believe the CIA's estimates that there were really 600,000 rather than 300,000 people in the communist forces. Nixon won because he promised a war-weary public he would bring peace with honor. Bush declared in October 2003 that "we're not leaving" Iraq soon, but his party and political advisers will probably have the last word as US casualties mount and his poll ratings continue to decline. Vietnam proved that the American public has limited patience. That is more the case than ever.

There is no evidence, either from the many first-hand memoirs or from the practice and conduct of American foreign policy since 1945, that grand policy options or goals were ever influenced or defined by information – nominally, analytic intelligence – that as truthfully as possible approximated reality in all its dimensions. Had this been the case, there would have been far fewer defeats and failures for Washington to confront, dealing with one mess after another, and the US would be a great deal more modest regarding its global interventions and ambitions. Respect for the parameters of reality involves decisive constraints, but the US simply does not decide its foreign policies this way. So what is the use and function of what is termed "intelligence" in the analytic meaning of that word?

The large technical and ideological cadres that purvey intelligence, rather than becoming a source of rationality and clarity, deluge an already inordinately complex foreign policy process with a huge quantity of data, and accurate information effectively becomes worthless as soon as it fails to reinforce what America's political and military leaders wish to hear. Intelligence functionaries accept the constraints of the system quite willingly because it pays their salaries. These personnel transform themselves into peddlers of just one more economic activity, and they never transcend the policy limits that the non-technocratic ruling elites impose. This is just as true in all areas of domestic affairs as in foreign policies.

The state's intelligence mechanisms are constrained by a larger structural and ideological environment and by the inherent irrationality of a foreign policy which foredooms any effort to base action on informed insight. Even when the insight is exact, and knowledge is far greater than ignorance, political and social boundaries usually place decisive limits on the application of "rationality" to actions. Political and ideological imperatives and interests – and, above all, careerism and the ambition to succeed by saying the "right" words – define the nature of the "relevant" truths. Intelligence's pretension to being objective is a hoax because those parts of it that do not reconfirm the power structure's interests and predetermined policies are ignored and discarded. There are innumerable reasons to reach this conclusion, not least because it has been confirmed by a growing number of insider memoirs and even by the official American intelligence community's own assessments. But more important is the entire experience in Iraq and the Americans' failed confrontation with the Islamic world for over half a century. To expect the US to behave otherwise than it has is to cultivate serious illusions and delude oneself.

The system, in a word, is irrational. We saw it in Vietnam and we are seeing it today in Iraq.

7
Technology and the Future of Warfare

The United States began to lose it scientific lead in the 1970s, and many of its Nobel Prize winners until then were refugees. Its technology has survived in large part because of the "brain drain" of foreigners to it. "I also think Western Europe is now our equal in some areas of science," the White House scientific adviser said in late 1979.[1] The American lead was always artificial.

Other nations had sufficient talent and retained it after economic conditions improved. The result was the equalization of technology and science, which can be used for many things: autos, steel, clothing, and the like, and eventually military technology was included. The US was the leader for a time, and the foreign-born scientists were crucial to its being the first to develop atomic bombs, but it gradually fell behind others. There were new competitors.

The consequence is the proliferation of scientific knowledge, which can be translated into automobiles or nuclear weapons – with every gradation in-between. That is exactly what has happened. Pakistan, working with China and North Korea, not only built its own nuclear bombs but will also sell the technology to build them to almost any nation that has the money – as early as 1988 it was ready to sell finished bombs to Saudi Arabia. The US would like to control its nuclear program lest Muslim terrorists, who have religious piety in common with many of its Muslim scientists, obtain a nuclear device and use it somewhere.

Both the United States and Russia have about 6,000 operational nuclear warheads each, but Israel has at least 60, perhaps 150, Pakistan and India about 110, North Korea up to 15. Nuclear proliferation is a fact of life. Many nations either have nuclear bombs already – made themselves or purchased – or the capacity to develop them. No one is quite sure how many, or which, countries have nuclear bombs already – the Israelis deny they have any. But the increased use of "traditional" weapons and explosives, which can be shoulder-carried or buried on roadsides, is now the principal danger facing the ascendant nations, of which the US remains the most important and aggressive.

These essays in this chapter deal with the lesser powers, but China has been developing its cyber warfare capacities for years and can neutralize America's space weapons with "cyber-worms." The Russians now claim to have a missile that can penetrate US anti-missile defenses. But poorer nations are more important because it is on their territory that the US is far more likely to fight. After all, America has fought weak and marginal nations since 1950, and it is the growing prowess of the poor, conducting guerilla and "Viet Cong" type warfare, that is of greatest importance. Israel's experience with Hizbollah or the US's abysmal failures in Afghanistan and Iraq prove that.

THE GREAT EQUALIZER:
LESSONS FROM IRAQ AND LEBANON
(Counterpunch, August 10, 2006)

The United States had a monopoly of nuclear weaponry only a few years before other nations challenged it, but from 1949 until 1991 deterrence theory worked – nations knew that if they used the awesome bomb they too were likely to be devastated in the inevitable riposte. Despite such examples of brinkmanship as the Cuban missile crisis and numerous threats of nuclear annihilation against non-nuclear powers, by and large the few nations that possessed the bomb concluded that nuclear war was not worth its horrendous risks.

Today, by contrast, weapons of mass destruction or precision and power are within the capacity of dozens of nations either to produce or purchase. With the multiplicity of weapons now available, deterrence theory is increasingly irrelevant and the equations of military power that existed in the period after World War II no longer hold. This process began in Korea after 1950, where the war ended in a standoff despite the nominal vast superiority of America's military power; likewise the Pentagon discovered that difficult terrain combined with guerilla tactics were more than a match for it in Vietnam, where the US was defeated. Both wars caused the US military and establishment strategists to reflect on the limits of high-tech warfare, and for a time it seemed as if appropriate lessons would be learned and costly errors not repeated.

The conclusion drawn from these major wars should have been that there were decisive limits to American military and political power, and that the US should drastically tailor its foreign policy to these limits and cease intervening anywhere it chose to. In short, it was necessary to accept the fact that it could not guide the world as it wished to. But such a conclusion, justified by experience, was far too radical for either Republicans or Democrats to fully embrace, and defense contractors never ceased promising the ultimate new weapon. America's leaders and military establishment argued in the wake of September 11 that technology would rescue it from further political failures. But such illusions – fed by the technological fetishism which is the hallmark of American civilization – led to the Iraq debacle.

There has now been a qualitative leap in technology that makes all inherited conventional wisdom, and war as an instrument of political policy, utterly irrelevant, not just to the US but to any other nation that embarks upon this course. Technology is now moving much faster than the political will to control its inevitable consequences – not to mention traditional strategic theories. Hizbollah has far better and more lethal rockets than it had a few years ago, and American experts believe that the Iranians compelled it to keep in reserve the far more powerful and longer range cruise missiles it already possesses. Iran itself possesses large quantities of these missiles and the experts believe they may very well be capable of destroying aircraft carrier battle groups. The Pentagon in August 2002, at a cost of $250 million, held a simulated war against Iran and lost it. Most of the American fleet was sunk. All attempts to devise defenses against speedboats armed with explosives and rockets failed. Technological devices to stop even the most primitive attacks have been expensive failures, and anti-missile technology everywhere has remained unreliable, even after decades of effort and billions of dollars spent.[2]

Even more ominous, the US army has just released a report that light water reactors – which 25 nations, from Spain to

Armenia and Slovenia, already have and which are covered by
no existing arms control treaties – can be used to obtain near
weapons-grade plutonium easily and cheaply. Within a few
years, many more countries than the present ten or so – the
army study thinks Saudi Arabia and even Egypt most likely –
will have nuclear bombs and far more destructive and accurate
rockets and missiles. If they have the money, then nuclear
designs and the weapons themselves can be purchased – and
probably have been already. Weapons-poor fighters will have
far more sophisticated guerilla tactics as well as far more lethal
equipment, which deprives the heavily equipped and armed
nations of the advantages of their overwhelming firepower, as
demonstrated in Afghanistan and Iraq. The battle between a
few thousand Hizbollah fighters and a massive, ultramodern
Israeli army backed and financed by the US proves this. Among
many other things, the war in Lebanon in the summer of 2006
was a window on the future. The outcome suggests that either
the Israelis cease their policy of destruction and intimidation,
and accept the political prerequisites of peace with the Arab
world, or they too will eventually be devastated by cheaper
and more accurate missiles and nuclear weapons in the hands
of at least two Arab nations and Iran.

What is now occurring in the Middle East reveals lessons
which will be just as relevant in the future to festering problems
in East Asia, Latin America, Africa, and elsewhere. Access to
nuclear weapons, cheap missiles and anti-personnel and anti-
vehicle bombs of greater portability and accuracy, and the
inherent limits of all antimissile systems, will set the context
for whatever crises arise in North Korea, Iran, Taiwan ... or
Venezuela. Trends which increase the limits of technology in
warfare are not only applicable to relations between nations
but also to groups within them – ranging from small con-

spiratorial entities up to large guerilla movements. The events in the Middle East have proven that warfare has changed dramatically everywhere, and that American hegemony can now be successfully challenged throughout the globe.

American power has been dependent to a large extent on its highly mobile navy. But ships are increasingly vulnerable to missile attack, and while they are a long way from being obsolete they are more-and-more circumscribed tactically and, ultimately, strategically. The Pentagon war games against Iran resulted in 16 major American boats being lost to armed speedboats. There is now a greater balance of power militarily, the reemergence of a kind of deterrence that means all future wars will be increasingly protracted, expensive, and very costly politically to leaders who blunder into wars under the illusion that offensives will be short and decisive. Olmert will eventually lose power in Israel, and destroying Lebanon will not save his political future. This too is a message not likely to be lost on politicians.

To this extent, what is emerging is a new era of more equal rivals. Enforceable universal disarmament of every kind of weapon would be far preferable. But short of this presently unattainable goal, the creation of a new equivalency is a vital factor leading less to peace in the real meaning of that term than perhaps to greater prudence. Such restraint could be an important factor leading to less war.

We live with twenty-first century technology but also with primitive political attitudes, nationalisms of assorted sorts, and cults of heroism and irrationality existing across the political and power spectrum. The world will destroy itself unless it realistically confronts the new technological equations. Israel must now accept this reality, and if it does not develop the political skills required to make serious compromises, the new equation suggests that it will be liquidated even as it rains destruction on its enemies. An increasing number of people in Israel realize this, although they are still a minority.

This is the message of the conflicts in Gaza, the West Bank, and Lebanon – to cite only the examples in today's papers. Walls are no longer protection for the Israelis – one shoots over them. Their much-vaunted Merkava tanks have proven highly vulnerable to new weapons that are becoming more and more common and are soon likely to be in Palestinian hands as well. At least 20 of these tanks were seriously damaged or destroyed in Lebanon in the 2006 war Israel initiated.

The US war in Iraq against the guerillas is a political disaster – a half-trillion dollars spent there, at the very least, and an even longer protracted war in Afghanistan have left America on the verge of defeat in both places. The "shock and awe" military strategy has utterly failed save to produce contracts for weapons makers – indeed, it has also contributed heavily to de facto economic bankruptcy in the US.

The Bush Administration has deeply alienated more of America's nominal allies than any US government in modern times. The Iraq War and subsequent conflict in Lebanon have left its Middle East policy in shambles and made Iranian strategic predominance far more likely, even inevitable – all of which was predicted before the Iraq invasion. US coalitions, as Thomas Ricks shows in his wordy but utterly convincing and critical book, *Fiasco: The American Military Adventure in Iraq*, are finished. America's sublime confidence and reliance on the power of its awesome weaponry is a crucial cause of its failure, although we cannot minimize its preemptory hubris and nationalist myopia. The United States, whose increasingly costly political and military adventures since 1950 have ended in failure, now must face the fact that the technology for confronting its power is rapidly becoming widespread and cheap. This technology is within the reach not merely of states but of relatively small groups of people. Destructive power is now virtually "democratized."[3]

DEFEAT: RUMSFELD AND THE AMERICAN WAY OF WAR
(Counterpunch, December 20, 2006)

It is relatively easy to comprehend the thinking, motives, and ideas of those who embark on wars. At the inception of conflicts, all advocates of war appear very similar, regardless of time and place, and a simplistic euphoric optimism suffuses their thinking. They expect triumph and glory, not ashes. More than in most nations, however, optimism is integral to the American creed.

Defeat is a wholly different matter. Denial, fantasy, illusion, and wish fulfillment – how do politicians confront failure? They find it too difficult to face the enormous damage they have done and the immense losses they have brought about. If the rulers of Germany, Russia, Japan, Italy, and elsewhere had known the momentous social and political costs their wars would entail, they surely would have been far more reluctant to embark on adventures that were to bring their societies to an end and radically change much of the history of the past century.

Disjunction and irrationality become the norm in these kinds of situations, and responses that seem bizarre are fairly predictable. Rationality often disappears in this process, and denial – and delay – becomes the norm. That is happening now in Washington, and probably in London and Canberra as well, because Bush's foreign policy has produced an immense disaster and there is less peace and stability in the world or security at home than at any time since 1945. Donald Rumsfeld's December 15th farewell speech as Defense Secretary should be read in this light, but also as a reflection of the much larger problem of the way US foreign and military policy has been conducted for decades. It is probably the precursor of those we have yet to hear – and will. If his speech were not so important it would be simply pathetic.

Rumsfeld: "Shock and Awe"

Rumsfeld is one of the most articulate advocates of the two major wars the US has embarked upon since 2000, and he had earlier made it plain to George Bush when he took office as Secretary of Defense that he would be "forward-leaning." Retribution for September 11 was an opportunity to realize dreams of heroism and success. He and Vice-President Dick Cheney are soul mates, and their careers have been intertwined, but Cheney seeks to keep out of the limelight while Rumsfeld adored the publicity that his cleverness attracted. He is best known for his desire to make the military both meaner and leaner, relying on high-tech solutions rather than manpower, and "shock and awe" became his slogan. But to realize these goals, national defense spending, which had been stable in the 1990s, increased from $294 billion in 2000 to $536 billion in 2006, and as a percentage of GNP it grew 37 percent from 2000 to 2006. All kinds of weapons, many the futuristic products of junk science concocted by well-placed manufacturers, were funded for eventual production – a dozen years being a short delivery time for many of them.

Rumsfeld's military dream was technology-intensive, even more so than 40 years ago, and it failed abysmally in Iraq. Army manpower, however, was reduced and forces were left unprepared in multiple domains, underfunded and overstretched even before the Iraq War began. Since then, the military's "readiness" in terms of available troops and equipment has only fallen precipitously. And while Rumsfeld made the army his enemy, even the air force now has to cut manpower to raise funds for new equipment.

Rumsfeld always premised his ambition, as various defense secretaries had attempted before him and failed, on the notion that the secret of military success was better and more weapons – "more bang for the buck" as an illustrious predecessor phrased it. More bucks also ensured that the Pentagon requests appeared much more palatable to a pork-hungry Congress eager to increase spending in their districts. Politics and complex diplomacy never interested people like Rumsfeld, even after the abysmal failure of the Vietnam War. Delivering bad news, which meant serious assessments, was the best way not to advance in the hierarchy, and careerism was a crucial factor in what people said. The name of the game was the game.

In both Afghanistan and Iraq Rumsfeld learned that reality was far more complex, and he managed to shock and awe both himself and the neoconservatives who shared his naive assumptions. Reliance on high-tech weaponry did not prevent warfare from becoming protracted, but it guaranteed that it would become far more costly. Both wars produced stalemates that have become the prelude to the defeats now staring the Bush Administration in the face.

Rumsfeld showed at various times that in certain ways he was a person of superior intelligence, notwithstanding the basically erroneous premises of the military system he led and the imperatives of ambition that required him to share them. But like his peers, he learned far too slowly. He suffered from the typical contradiction between intelligence and ambition, and the latter requires an ideology and assumptions which most men of power come to believe.

His November 6, 2006 memo on the Iraq War admitted that "what US forces are currently doing in Iraq is not working well enough or fast enough." There were some anodynes he advocated too, but it was rightly interpreted as his concession to the Baker–Hamilton panel view, the voice of the traditional foreign policy Establishment, that the Iraq War was going disastrously – in effect, was being lost. Since then, former Secretary of State Colin L. Powell has declared there is a civil war raging in Iraq and that there should be a drawdown of American troops, to begin by the middle of 2007 – a step that even Rumsfeld favored with modest withdrawals that would compel the Iraqis "to pull up their socks."

Rumsfeld and his peers know the US military cannot win the war in Iraq. Just as during the Vietnam War, they have the quixotic hope that a political solution for the profound and bloody turmoil that reigns there can be found. At first the Shiites, Sunnis, and Kurds were to have parliamentary elections and make a political deal. They did not. Then they were to write a constitution, which they eventually managed to do but it changed nothing. Now they are hoping that the prime minister, Nouri al-Maliki, can miraculously cobble together some kind of consensus that will produce peace. But Bush's closest advisers think it is very likely he will fail. They have no one else to turn to. Politics, like military power, will not prevent the United States from losing control over events in Iraq – thereby losing the war. A "surge" in American troops in Iraq, as even the Joint Chiefs of Staff now argue, is only a recipe for greater disasters. Attacks against US coalition forces, their Iraqi dependents, and civilians have now reached a peak and are at over twice the level of two years ago. The Bush Administration today confronts disaster in Iraq, and probably the worst foreign policy failure in American history. Futility is the hallmark of all its efforts.

Rumsfeld's Final Thoughts

Rumsfeld's farewell speech is therefore all the more remarkable because it attempts to revive older notions, long discredited and seriously at odds with facts that he himself accepted only weeks earlier. It represents a type of recidivism that is all too common when disaster approaches, and it reveals the kind of intellectual schizophrenia that afflicts those who rise to the top. It is a symptom of the complete failure of the crew that has led the US for the past six years, and their total inability to confront reality.

Rumsfeld's final words are Soviet-centric, and he reiterated his 1977 declaration that "weakness is provocative." If "aggressors" in our "new era" perceive weakness or a lack of resolution they will be enticed "into acts they otherwise would avoid." But "the enemy" consists of "unstable dictators, weapons proliferators and rogue regimes" ready to use "unconventional" and "irregular" threats. They mix "extremist ideology" with modern weaponry. The "perception of weakness" is provocative, as is the "reluctance to defend our way of life." The unnamed enemy is resolved to destroy "freedom." Concretely, Rumsfeld thinks the US should "invest more" to protect itself.

His mélange includes a theory of US military credibility, a notion that got America into the Vietnam debacle. Credibility is certainly now a factor in the Iraq and Afghan wars, one shared by many administration leaders. Rumsfeld does not confront the fact that persisting until utter defeat will make the US look not credible but dangerously irrational. His speech is historically and factually wholly inaccurate. It ignores entirely the fact that the existence of WMD in Saddam Hussein's hands was used as an excuse for the Iraq War but none were ever found. Many of the unstable dictators, rogue regimes, Islamic fundamentalists, and their ilk were useful allies in the US confrontation with the USSR and communism, and America gave them both weapons and training. This policy was bipartisan, pursued by Democrats as enthusiastically as by Republicans, and reflects the consensus which the Bush Administration shares with its predecessors, a fact that explains why the Democrats refuse to break with the President's wars.

Had the US not intervened covertly and overtly after 1947 to undermine the many regimes it thought dangerous, even though most were neutralist, reformist, and legitimate, there would be far fewer extremists today for it to worry about. But that they now pose some sort of fatal danger to the United States is a sheer fantasy that the Bush Administration has concocted to justify a foreign policy the American people now reject.

Rumsfeld's final speech bears no relation whatever to the situation the US now confronts, not just in the Middle East but everywhere. Like the President and those around him, it refuses to confront reality.

The American Way of War

The fact is that the immense and costly American military today bears no relationship to politics and reality. It accounts for nearly half of the world's military expenditure but it cannot win its two current wars against the most primitive enemies, enemies themselves divided into multiple factions who often fight each other more than they do the Americans and who could not care less what Washington spends on weaponry and manpower. But America's leaders have always assumed they are dealing with convenient enemies, who calculate the way the US wants them to. More importantly, the politics of war was never adequately addressed; it existed as an afterthought and never interfered with fighting and winning the American way. The Soviet Union and communism no longer exist, and yet absolutely nothing has changed in America's behavior and thinking. The Pentagon is superb at spending money but its way of warfare is now in a profound and perhaps terminal crisis. It has lost all its wars against persistent guerillas armed with cheap, light weapons who decentralize and hide effectively.

The military system that Rumsfeld and his precursors created is increasingly dysfunctional and fit only to suit the expensive demands and pretensions of the powerful companies in the military-industrial complex. The emphasis on expensive weaponry is good for the US economy; successful counter-insurgency warfare costs too little to maintain full employment. It bears scant relationship to the political problems the US has confronted for decades – and now more than ever.

America's weapons are made to fight state-centric wars and destroy concentrated targets – they were designed originally for the USSR and its Warsaw bloc allies, and for European conditions. Confronting China demanded some minor modifications in this strategy. Even ignoring that nuclear deterrence made this emphasis irrelevant, or that the Korean and Vietnam wars proved it was destined to fail, it took (and still takes) 15 to 20 years to develop and produce the kind of equipment the US has always fetishized.

But communism has disappeared in Europe and in all but name in China. The budgeting cycle, which keeps the economy of the US buoyant and is deftly spread to numerous Congressional districts, bears no relation to American foreign policy, which makes former friends foes, ex-foes allies and members of NATO, and changes every few years like a kaleidoscope. As a very recent study for the US Army Strategic Studies Institute concludes, "the United States [is] prepared to fight the most dangerous but least likely threats and unprepared to fight the least dangerous but most likely threats."[4] The American way of war is technology intensive, firepower focused, logistically superior but politically and culturally ignorant to the point of being pathetic.

Rumsfeld did not initiate this myopia, which has been inherent in US foreign and military policies since 1947, regardless of whether Democrats or Republicans were in power. He only attempted to apply it to Afghan and Iraqi conditions, to sand and heat, to profoundly divided places, and he has only continued the legacy of failures that began long ago.

Hence defeat.

Conclusion

My conclusion is that there is no conclusion. Change is now the motif of human history. Communism and socialism have fallen, and just as capitalism seems to have triumphed it has made instability intrinsic to its very system. The spread of nuclear weaponry to many, perhaps dozens, of nations, and the equalization of military technology have made warfare more likely and more awesome than ever. Now wars will be between equals who can destroy one another. In short, it is a moment of great danger, and the only thing that seems certain is that the century of American supremacy is now ending.

The world is changing at an exponential rate. Since at least 1945 we have been living through an extremely rapid transformation. All the old verities and ideas have disappeared and proved irrelevant, not only Leftist concepts as the communist and social democrat parties throughout the world declined, but also those of the mainstream who have ruled most nations for over a century and who had tremendous, unquestioning self-confidence.

No sooner than a specific event occurs and news of it is printed, whether about politics or the economy, it is outdated – almost on a daily basis. Some American leaders now pine for a return to the stability which the USSR and communism provided, and nations that call themselves "communist" – like China – are rescuing capitalism at a time when it is experiencing a financial crisis that may turn out to be the worst it has undergone since the Great Depression of 1929. There are certainly dominant trends but they remain largely inexplicable, and now no one on the Left, Right, or that painfully nebulous category, the Center, has the pretension to explain them with confidence. That, in itself, reflects the collapse of all ideas and notions of humanity's fate.

With ironies and changes of a magnitude that seem virtually limitless, with transformations everywhere that are increasingly rapid, complex, and confusing, we must now confront a bewildering reality that exceeds our comprehension – and that of those who have always ruled nations. But comprehend we must – hence these random thoughts, many of them dated almost as soon as they were written, about some of the critical dimensions of the world we live in. We still must think, and attempt to confront reality.

If history proves nothing else, it is that politics and the human experience are entirely unpredictable – surprise and change is the essence of the fate of every people and nation.

There are countless challenges confronting mankind, many of them technical. Nuclear proliferation, the role of India and China as a counterbalance to US military and economic power, what the price of food and commodities – especially petroleum – will do to the global balance of economic and political power, and the like. This book touches only on some of them, but the subjects here are scarcely trivial. They are crucial and bear on the future of US power and the premises that have driven it historically and especially since 1945 – America's period of consummate hubris and pretension.

What is certain is that American power is now declining everywhere, leading to a shift in the global role it played from

1945 to 1991, when the alleged Soviet menace disappeared. The US invested trillions of dollars in technologies for which there is no use since the formal absence of a technologically sophisticated enemy. The disappearance of the USSR in 1991 has left the US endowed with exceptionally expensive weapons, nuclear bombs and delivery systems, and a useless but highly funded air arm equipped with irrelevant destructive hardware. The absence of real identifiable foes has been a disaster, leaving the US aimless – it picks and chooses enemies: rag-tag Afghan tribesmen, Iraqis of all sorts, perhaps China, perhaps Russia again but now without Bolsheviks, South American caudillos, small groups of conspirators whose reach spreads across borders and whose nationalities are obscure ... the choices are now limitless. The US needs real, identifiable enemies, not legacies of the Cold War.

Never before have the limits of America's power and ambition, transcending "communism" and history as it was from 1917 to 1991, been more evident. The US must accept the political and military consequences of the fact that the world is no longer dependent on its economic might, as it was after 1945, and that the hubris and ambitions it developed then are increasingly irrelevant. Indeed, it has to recognize that there are now other nations with an economic power equaling or even, in the near future, exceeding its own. It is today dependent on the world economy, which it once dominated, and on nations that have their own power.

What might replace American power is also in transition. What will happen next? Will China and India become more powerful than the US? All of America's alliances, which we no longer remember, from CENTO to SEATO, have disappeared, and so will NATO. Are commodity prices – now skyrocketing and the basis of burgeoning Russian and Middle Eastern wealth and political influence – the result of real trends or of speculators' interventions? How far will nuclear arms proliferation go? Will Japan become a nuclear power? – there are those there ready to embrace the possibility. Will there be a nuclear war, which would make everything we think is important seem meaningless? This is probably the most serious danger facing the world today, and the most crucial aspect of my essay on the spread of military technology to poor nations.

What comes next is sheer guesswork. What began as a problem with the sub-prime mortgage market may lead to economic perturbations or crises of an untold magnitude. The world's economy is in a structurally new situation – only time will tell what it means. As a result of "globalization" and "free markets" – the Washington consensus – the economies of the world are interlocked in a way unique in recent history. And this equalization of economic practices poses potentially great dangers. No one knows – neither those who lead nor critics like myself. But crucial though the world economy is, there is far more for the United States to worry about.

Who would have imagined a few years ago that the cost of food and commodities, which has increased enormously, would make social instability in much of the poorer world far greater than when communist agitators were still active? Increasing the price of food for the masses is the surest way to bring about the overthrow of societies, but now there is no organized force to lead them. The result will be diverse forms of protest, each under different auspices – leading perhaps to chaos rather than communism. Perhaps new forms of opposition that we are unable to imagine – whether religiously inspired or secular – will emerge.

The historic opposition – made up of communists and socialists – has disappeared, its credibility gone. What will replace it? There will certainly be an opposition because conditions – of inequality and social injustice, global warming, instability and war, hunger, unemployment, etc. – still warrant it. The exact nature of this opposition is at present a mystery, but we will have a new resistance whatever form it takes.

Unless a force arises to replace the traditional socialists, the economy will produce "crises" only in the sense that bankers lose money, going from one "crisis" to another. What will follow the "socialists" is yet to be resolved – but only the arrival of a force to replace socialism will create a real crisis because, despite the massive losses, capitalism will endure far longer in the absence of a movement that seeks to abolish it.

President George W. Bush hardly initiated the decline of American power – which began after the Korean War, was continued in relation to Cuba, and was greatly accelerated in Vietnam – but he has done much to exacerbate it further. In no place in the world is American power now hegemonic – including the Western Hemisphere, which I have not discussed here, but deal with in other books. The world is going very badly for the United States – everywhere, in the economic as well as political and military domains. Its power is in the process of being reversed. There will be other unforeseen crises to challenge American power, and they may occur on any continent.

Its century of domination is now ending.

Notes

Introduction

1. Zbigniew Brzezinski on the BBC, February 1, 2008, as printed in *The Spokesman*, 99.
2. Donald M. Wilber, *Regime Change in Iran: Overthrow of Premier Mossadeq of Iran, November 1952–August 1953*, Nottingham: Bertrand Russell Peace Foundation, 2006, pp. 70–1. This is an official secret British history first published in 1969.

1 The Financial Crisis

1. International Monetary Fund, *World Economic Outlook*, April 2008, pp. xi, xviii.
2. *IMF Survey*, May 29, 2006; http://www.imf.org/external/pubs/ft/survey/2006/052906.pdf. *IMF in Focus*, September 2006; http://www.imf.org/external/pubs/ft/survey/2006/090106.pdf
3. Roberto Zagha, "Rethinking Growth," *Finance & Development*, Washington DC, March 2006; http://www.imf.org/external/pubs/ft/fandd/2006/03/zagha.htm. Stephen Roach, *Global Economic Forum*, Morgan Stanley, New York, June 16, 2006. http://www.morganstanley.com/GEFdata/digests/20060616-fri.html
4. *Financial Times*, July 17 and August 14, 2006.
5. Garry J. Schinasi, *Safeguarding Financial Stability: Theory and Practice*, Washington: IMF, 2006; http://www.imf.org/External/Pubs/NFT/2005/SFS/eng/sfs.pdf#search=%22Safeguarding%20Financial%20Stability%3A%20Theory%20and%20Practice%22. The term "Washington consensus" was coined by the economist John Williamson in 1989 and summarizes the recommendations made to states, including tax reductions, free markets, privatization and financial deregulation. To qualify for IMF loans, governments must implement such measures.
6. This and following quotes are from Schinasi, *Safeguarding Financial Stability*.

7. Kern Alexander, Rahul Dhumale and John Eatwell, *Global Governance of Financial Systems: The International Regulation of Systemic Risk*, Oxford: Oxford University Press, 2005.

8. *Financial Times*, July 27, 2006.

9. With assets of only $5 billion, LTCM found itself owing some $100 billion. The Federal Reserve and Wall Street paid out $3.6 billion to prevent the system from collapsing.

10. As with all derivatives, operators bet on foreseeable risks, but in this case it was credit (bonds, debts, etc.) that was exchanged.

11. The seller undertakes, subject to payment of a surcharge, to compensate the customer in the event of a default on payment or simply a deterioration in the quality of its debtors.

12. Gillian Tett, "The dream machine, invention of credit derivatives," *Financial Times Magazine*, March 24–25, 2006; *Financial Times*, July 10 and 19, 2006, August 14, 24 and 29, 2006.

13. *Financial Times*, June 23, and 24–25, 2006.

14. See Tom Frank, "Enron: Elvis lives," *Le Monde diplomatique*, English language edition, February 2002.

15. *Financial Times*, May 31, June 8, July 17, 2006.

16. Amaranth, based in Connecticut, incurred huge losses speculating on the price of natural gas. Brian Hunter, the energy trader said to be largely responsible for the losses, was later said to have left the company; at the same time, the company's chief executive officer, Nick Maounis, told investors that it planned to get out of energy trading, in which it had previously invested more than half its capital.

17. With these loans it is possible to buy a company with a very small capital outlay and loans at rates lower than the expected rate of profit.

18. *Global Economic Forum*, Morgan Stanley, April 24, 2006.

19. Ibid., June 23, September 5, 2006.

20. *Financial Times*, September 6, 2006.

21. Alexander, Dhumale and Eatwell, *Global Governance*, passim.

22. Bank for International Settlements, 76th Annual Report, Basel, June 26, 2006; http://www.bis.org/publ/annualreport.htm

23. Ibid.

2 The Contours of Recent American Foreign Policy

1. Michael Beschloss and Strobe Talbott, *At the Highest Levels: The Inside Story of the End of the Cold War*, Boston: Little, Brown, 1993, pp. 106, 346; US Joint Chiefs of Staff, *1991 Joint Military Net Assessment*, Washington DC, March 1991, pp. 1–2.
2. David Fromkin, *A Peace to End All Peace: The Fall of the Ottoman Empire and the Creation of the Modern Middle East*, New York: Henry Holt, 1989, p. 262.

3 Alliances and NATO

1. Joseph E. Stiglitz, *The Roaring Nineties: A New History of the World's Most Prosperous Decade*, New York: Norton, 2003, passim.
2. Gabriel Kolko, *Another Century of War?*, New York: New Press, 2004, passim.
3. Zbigniew Brzezinski, *The Choice: Global Domination or Global Leadership*, New York: Basic Books, 2004, passim.
4. Pew Research Center, "A Year After the Iraq War," March 16, 2004.
5. Wade Boese, "Russia, NATO at Loggerheads Over Military Bases," *Arms Control Today*, March 2004; *Los Angeles Times*, March 26, 2004.
6. Dr. Stephen J. Blank, "Toward a New US Strategy in Asia," US Army Strategic Studies Institute, February 24, 2004.

4 Israel: A Stalemated Accident of History

1. George Tenet, *At the Center of the Storm: My Years at the CIA*, New York: HarperCollins, 2007 p. 54.
2. Benedict Anderson, *Imagined Communities: Reflections on the Origin and Spread of Nationalism*, London: Verso, 1983, pp. 4–6.
3. David Fromkin, *A Peace to End All Peace: The Fall of the Ottoman Empire and the Creation of the Modern Middle East*, New York: Henry Holt, 1989, pp. 272–3, 278, 317.
4. William M. Johnston, *The Austrian Mind: An Intellectual and Social History, 1848–1938*, Berkeley: University of California

Press, 1972, pp. 357–61; Yuri Slezkine, *The Jewish Century*, Princeton: Princeton University Press, 2004, pp. 149–52; Fromkin, *A Peace to End All Peace*, pp. 272, 294.

5. Slezkine, *The Jewish Century*, passim.

6. Data on Palestine from Population of Ottoman and Mandate Palestine: Statistical and Demographic Considerations, 2002–5, pp. 5, 6, 11 and passim; http://www.mideastweb.org/palpop. htm

7. The early 2008 Gaza conflicts later confirmed this but Olmert and his generals very likely expected to secure a great victory within five days, thereby increasing his popularity with the hawkish Jewish population that forms a growing majority of the voters, to reverse his abysmally low poll ratings, thereby saving his political career (he received a 3 percent popularity rating in a TV poll in early March 2007).

8. In late April 2008, with Bush and Rice about to visit the region, and progress in negotiations between Israel and the Palestinians locked in what is now the traditional impasse, Olmert completely reversed his position on a Syrian peace deal. It remains to be seen if anything comes of what appears to this writer like a ploy to give the US a claim to have accomplished something positive in the Middle East during the President's final months in office. The Americans are still opposed to a Syria–Israel peace accord.

6 The Limits of Intelligence

1. Gabriel Kolko and Joyce Kolko, *The Limits of Power: The World and United States Foreign Policy, 1945–1954*, New York: Harper & Row, 1972, pp. 339–42.

2. Willard C. Matthias, *America's Strategic Blunders: Intelligence Analysis and National Security Policy, 1936–1991*, University Park: Pennsylvania State University Press, 2001, p. 3. See also ibid., pp. 45–6 for a 1946 estimate of Soviet intentions.

3. Ibid., p. 3.

4. Ibid., p. 313. See also Robert M. Gates, *From the Shadows: The Ultimate Insider's Story of Five Presidents and How They Won the Cold War*, New York: Simon & Schuster, 1996, pp. 30–1.

5. Gates, *From the Shadows*, p. 207.

6. Ibid., p. 286.
7. George W. Allen, *None So Blind: a Personal Account of Intelligence Failure in Vietnam*, Chicago: Ivan R. Dee, Inc., 2001, p. 78.
8. Ibid., pp. 183, 185.
9. Jeffrey Race, "The Unlearned Lessons of Vietnam," *Yale Review*, LXVI (1976), pp. 163–6, 173.
10. Harold P. Ford, *CIA and the Vietnam Policymakers: Three Episodes 1962–1968*, Washington, DC: CIA Center for the Study of Intelligence, 1998; http://www.odci.gov/csi/books/vietnam/index.html
11. Allen, *None So Blind*, p. 248.
12. Ibid., p. 266.
13. Ibid., p. 235
14. Ibid., p. 242.
15. Ibid., p. 267.
16. Steven R. Ward, "Evolution Beats Revolution in Analysis," *Studies in Intelligence* (CIA Center for the Study of Intelligence), vol. 46, no. 3, 2002; http://www.odci.gov/csi/studies/vol46no3/article04.html. See also CIA, Center for the Study of Intelligence, "Roundtable Report, Intelligence and Policy: The Evolving Relationship, November 10, 2003," Washington, DC, June 2004, pp. 7–8.
17. See, for example, John T. Carney and Benjamin F. Schemmer, *No Room for Error: The Covert Operations of America's Special Tactics Units from Iran to Afghanistan*, New York: Ballantine Books, 2002; and Robert Baer, *See No Evil: The True Story of a Ground Soldier in the CIA's War on Terrorism*, New York: Crown Publisher, 2002; Elaine Grossman, "Combat Commanders Make Broad Access to Intelligence a Top Priority," *Inside the Pentagon*, February 9, 2006.
18. CIA, "Intelligence and Policy," p. 14 and passim.
19. Scott Ritter, *Iraq Confidential: The Untold Story of the Intelligence Conspiracy to Undermine the UN and Overthrow Saddam Hussein*, New York: Nation Books, 2005, pp. 9ff., 75, 112–13, 289–91.
20. Paul R. Pillar, "Intelligence, Policy, and the War in Iraq," *Foreign Affairs*, 85 (March/April 2006), passim. Pillar was the CIA's

National Intelligence Officer for the Near East, 2000–5; he criticizes every premise of the Administration's Iraq policy and shows how the CIA disproved every one of them – to no effect. See also *New York Times*, November 6, 2005; AFP dispatch, November 24, 2005; Michel R. Gordon and Bernard E. Trainor, *Cobra II: The Inside Story of the Invasion and Occupation of Iraq*, New York: Pantheon Books, 2006, pp. 126–7.

21. Bob Woodward, *Plan of Attack*, New York: Simon & Schuster, 2004, p. 19.

22. Bob Drogin and John Goetz, "The Curveball Saga," *Los Angeles Times*, November 20, 2005; James Risen, *State of War: The Secret History of the CIA and the Bush Administration*, New York: Free Press, 2006, pp. 72–6, 102–3; *Washington Post*, April 9, 2006.

23. Three National Security Archives releases, October 21, 2005; one NSA release, April 7, 2006. See also Anonymous (Mike Scheuer), *Imperial Hubris: Why the West is Losing the War on Terror*, Washington, DC: Brassey's, 2004; James Bamford, *A Pretext for War: 9/11, Iraq, and the Abuse of America's Intelligence Agencies*, New York: Doubleday, 2004; Pillar, "Intelligence, Policy, and the War in Iraq," passim.

24. David Talbot, "How Technology Failed in Iraq," *Technology Review* (MIT), November 2004, p. 2 and passim; http://www.techreview.com/Hardware/wtr_13893,294,p1.html

25. Gabriel Kolko, *Anatomy of a War: Vietnam, the United States, and the Modern Historical Experience*, New York: The New Press, 1994, pp. 49–50. See ibid., passim, for the Vietnam War in general.

26. Angus Reid polls, November 14, 2005; February 24, 2006; March 2, 2006; Fox News, April 20, 2006. Polls that frame questions differently get different figures but all show that an increasing majority feels that the Iraq War was an error. See Program on International Policy Attitudes (PIPA) poll, ca. March 15, 2006, which claims only 26 percent want all troops withdrawn within six months.

27. *USA Today*, October 23, 2003.

7 Technology and the Future of Warfare

1. *International Herald Tribune*, October 30, 1979.
2. Mark Williams, "The Missiles of August: The Lebanon War and the Democratization of Missile Technology," *Technology Review*, August 16, 2006.
3. For another compelling dimension of the more level playing field in battlefield communications, see Iason Athanasiadis, "How Hi-tech Hezbollah called the Shots," *Asia Times*, September 9, 2006.
4. Kevin Reynolds, *Defense Transformation: To What, for What?*, US Army War College, November 21, 2006, p. x.

Index

Compiled by Sue Carlton